An Apologia for Christian Identity

Writings of Pastor Mark Downey

James N. Jester, Editor

James Nelson Publications
TRUTH MATTERS

ISBN-13: 9781795840309

All Bible quotations from KJV unless otherwise noted.

This book printed in the United States of America.

This book available at Amazon.com or may be ordered at any bookstore. To order additional copies of this book contact James Nelson Publications at cedarridgenorth@yahoo.com

CONTENTS

Dedication

To my parents who ingrained upon me at an early age the love of truth, and to the spiritually blinded majority of Israelite kinsmen in New JerUSAlem. As Noah warned his fellows of the impending flood, may this book serve as a signpost of the times.

Acknowledgments

I would like to acknowledge the faithful encouragement of my wife, Debbie, who has urged me to be all that I am and do all that I can, including publishing books such as this.

FOREWORD

It is with great honor that I present to you this book of sermons and messages from the late pastor Mark W. Downey (1949-2018). During his last years (2015-2018), he served at the Fellowship of God's Covenant People church, where he delivered these timely sermons. Mark truly had a way with words; and was a great stalwart for the Truth, as found in the Word of God.

His web site, KinsmanRedeemer.com, still remains active at the time of this writing and was the source for the production of this book.

James N. Jester, Editor

INTRODUCTION

Christian Identity - What Is It?

"For thou art an holy people unto the Lord thy God: the Lord thy God hath chosen thee to be a special people unto himself, above all people that are upon the face of the earth." —Deuteronomy 7:6

As the word identity implies, it is the condition of being the same as something described or asserted. Christian Identity establishes who the true Israel is today according to the Holy Bible and world history. There is more than adequate and convincing proof that the Anglo-Saxon, Celtic, Scandinavian, Germanic and kindred peoples are the racial descendants of the tribes of Israel.

It becomes readily apparent that there has been a case of mistaken identity when associating Jews with the claim of being the "chosen people." The Jew has an identity, but it is that of a thief who has stolen the history and nomenclature of the true Hebrews and Semites. For the sake of understanding it is necessary to clearly distinguish between the terms Israel, Judah and Jewry, because of the careless, thoughtless and often purposely deceptive usage by both religious and political leaders.

The time has come when the hidden Israel nation is being revealed to those having eyes to see and ears to hear. It is being positively identified. Only one race answers to the Holy Bible scenario of

Israel in the latter days and that is the White Race. Our people are in possession of what Israel was to possess and we are doing what Israel was to do according to God's covenants and promises, which Christ came to confirm. Only our people have the Bible, believe in Jesus the Messiah, call on His Name, are called by His Name, have used His Laws for our civil government and are now the object of a worldwide attack by the enemies of Jesus Christ who are organizing all the heathen under the Red banner of antichrist World Communism.

In Genesis, God created Adam, the first man. The Holy Bible is a history book of Adam's people. The Hebrew word for man is Adam itself and actually means to show blood in the face; to be fair; rosy cheeked; to be ruddy; and to be able to blush or flush. One must admit that the other races do not fit this description and therefore, cannot descend through Adam. God declared, "Everything after its own kind." From Adam, there proceeded a chosen line who followed God after righteousness. From Adam's son Seth, to Noah the chosen line remained racially pure and faithful to God. Noah and his family were preserved during the Great Flood while God destroyed the disobedient. Noah's son, Shem, continued the chosen line and these people became known as Shemites or Semites.

Next was Eber, whose descendants became known as Hebrews. Generations later, God chose one Hebrew-Adamic man who remained faithful to God and did not live in wickedness, as did the other races. This was Abraham, who received special blessings and covenants from God. Abraham passed these blessings along to his son, Isaac who passed them on to his son Jacob. Jacob's name was changed to Israel and he had twelve sons, who then founded the twelve tribes of Israel. These tribes were disobedient to God's Laws and, in 745 BC, went into Assyrian captivity. From Assyria, these people migrated west and became the Caucasian European nations. The United States of America and Canada uniquely fulfill the prophesied place of the re-gathering of all the tribes of Israel.

The people of true Israel will recognize their identity and turn to the Lord Jesus Christ and call upon Him for Salvation and Redemption, and that they will be delivered from their enemies in the "last battle" which will destroy the wicked and will usher in the great Kingdom Age upon the earth.

"He sheweth his word unto Jacob, his statutes and his judgments unto Israel. He hath not dealt so with any nation; and as for his judgments they have not known them. Praise ye the Lord." –Psalm 147:19-20

Why We ARE Christian Identity

Regardless of what the jewish controlled news media says about Christian Identity, we most certainly are not going to put our tail between our legs and call ourselves something else. We are not dogs and we are not pusillanimous chameleons. The propaganda of antichrist scribes can throw their worst diatribes of slander at us and we will remain instruments of God's righteousness, while our adversaries remain vessels of dishonor.

If words can mutate into a negative connotation simply because there is no resistance to a style of linguistic alchemy, then we are at the mercy of sorcerers whose expertise is demonization. We will not surrender the God-given appellation of Identity, as something bad just because bad people call it that, anymore than the Protestants would have cowered to the power of the Pope.

In the war of words, in spiritual warfare, in the battle of ideas, the bottom line is the truth vs. the lie. It is difficult for most White people to fathom how much deceitfulness is incorporated into the people who hate us as their very way of life. Jewish communism has never made any bones about saying whatever it takes to destroy Christianity and western civilization. If, "for fear of the jews" (John 7:13) we change our divine designation to milquetoast reformers or Anglo separatists, it will only be a matter of time when the word 'Christian' is politically incorrect. Now is the time, in this generation, to stand up against these dens of vipers and "contend for the faith" (Jude 3).

The word Identity is the perfect reference to our Movement (Mt. 5:48). We not only identify our race as the true Israel, we put everything under the scriptural microscope with a Berean fervor (Acts 17:11). We are not an invention of the media to be manipulated unless we acquiesce with a whimper and say to the network tabloids "please don't call us Identity anymore." I have news for the antichrist that thinks their persecution will silence us. The good news is that there are still men of Israel who will stand in

9

the gap and with joy and gladness declare themselves Identity, not because they are iconoclastic idolaters or have a persecution complex, but rather because, "If God be for us, who can be against us?" –Romans 8:31.

It is blasphemy to suggest that jews espoused 'Identity' over 100 years ago, when in fact the pernicious misrepresentation has blurred the truth with what is known as British Israelism (during the time of Oliver Cromwell) to allow jews' reentry into England (after 300 years of a jew-free society). The term 'Identity' can be documented as having originated in the 1950s with William Potter Gale who was second-in-command to General Douglas MacArthur in the Pacific theater of post WWII. The professional liars have tried to denigrate MacArthur through character assassination (words), however, he remains a hero to many Americans. If the liars can criminalize patriotism, then it is perjury that is the crime, not the patriot.

The image-makers will reap what they sow. When our people wake up (and they will) to the fact that the two greatest movements for the preservation of our culture was German nationalism of the 1930's and the Reconstruction Klan after the War of Northern Aggression, then we as a people will be proud of our heritage and not ashamed of the media generated epithets. We shall relish and savor each slur as a badge of honor. We shall see the real purveyors of malice towards mankind when the words of the Anti Defamation League and Morris Dees fall on deaf ears. They will be cast out of our society and there shall be weeping and gnashing of teeth (Mt. 25:30).

The ADL is not going to define Identity for me, or my church. Fear mongers do not intimidate real Christians as to what they are or are not. Modern Pharisees create their own self-fulfilling prophecies. Eventually the pendulum of disgust will swing against them. As long as we have Christian watchmen watching the so called hate-group watchdogs and identify their every move, our Movement will advance. Our sights are on the Kingdom. God is in control. Identity is not the enemy of God's Kingdom.

We are a danger to wickedness in high places because the laws of God are in conflict with the laws of man. How much longer will we tolerate legalized plunder from a corrupt aristocracy of thieves?

When will we once again demand the sanity and government of Jesus Christ as our only salvation?

We are Christian Identity and will not let the sophistry of wolves in sheep's clothing dissuade us from our divine calling. We are called to identify the Truth. It is the Truth that shall make us free from the rhetoric of vain imaginations. There is nothing new under the sun. There are still those who want to play god and control every aspect of people's lives. Identity Christians simply want to worship our God in peace in our own Promised Land.

However, the words being leveled against Identity are to deny us our liberty. There will be those who try to destroy us from within, but we know them by their fruits. The Bible warns us about false brethren and false teachers. *"Professing themselves to be wise, they became fools"* (Romans 1:22). The only false identity is the White man that cannot look in a mirror and thank his Creator for all that He has given him. Our lost Identity, as God's redeemed people Israel is now found and declared. We are the 'Bride' of Christ. "Whom God has joined together let no man put asunder" (Mt. 19:6). *"And the gates of hell shall not prevail against it"* (Mt. 16:18).

Mark W. Downey

Chapter 1

By What Authority?

Back in the 1980's, every Friday night I would attend a tax protestors meeting in the basement of friends of mine and it got so popular, through word of mouth, that we were getting around 20 or more people at every meeting. We had wonderful discussions, mapping out strategies to defeat the IRS. I remember one of the key salvos in letters of response, was the question 'by what authority' do they compel Americans to comply with their codes, because there usually wasn't any. I learned what 'colorable law' meant. It's the conduct or action of somebody having governmental authority that is not within the law. Police issuing traffic tickets are probably the most common example of 'colorable law', because we have the right of mobility. Just because cars were invented, does that mean we gave somebody the authority to punish us for traveling without a permission card (license), that you have to pay for?

People pay taxes to a corporation that has nothing to do with America, land of the free. Around the same time our anti-tax group got going, we also started a church group in a log cabin that another church had vacated because of a split. There was quite a bit of discussion at that time about *authority* and the primary focus of the Christian Patriot movement, as it was called back then, and was understandably from a biblical perspective. There were a lot of good articles and books written about authority. There were some victories in the courts, but for the most part, these challenges to the system, to the Babylonian-Masonic way of doing things, were prosecuted and people went to jail. Some patriots were even murdered like Gordon Kahl. After so much blood, sweat and tears I think the movement lost its momentum and many people became despondent. But not me, especially when the government ramped up the stakes with Ruby Ridge, Waco and the Murrah Federal Building. And then, later with 9-11; and who knows what the next false flag operation will be. All of it designed to strengthen the power elite and vicarious authority of a colorable government, which even has its own colored president now.

Well, what prompted me to get on this subject has been a discussion I've been having on Stormfront, the world's largest racialist website with over 100,000 members, between believers and non-believers (including pagans, agnostics and atheists). There's quite a mixture of reaction to Christian Identity, from admiration to raw hatred. The movement has moved from the streets and courts to the Internet, and is now called the White Nationalist movement and is arbitrarily declared *secular*. Think about it: Jesus Christ has been removed as the preeminent figurehead for White people desperately concerned about their children's future. Fortunately, White Nationalism is not the only movement for White people seeking answers to our problems. Hence, the clash between the Christian Identity movement and them.

Let me give you a sampling of the dialogue and we'll see how it evolved into a question of authority. An atheist with an open mind said, "Let's face it, Christian Identity could be a major part of breaking the chains of Zionism, yet we fail to support them in a meaningful way, because we are selfish and put our personal feelings before our race. That's the way I see it, and I don't care [about those] who don't like it; and Christian Identity is correct in saying there are a few [posters and moderators] blocking any meaningful activism of Christian Identity on this website." How's that for an endorsement, and from an atheist!

13

There are other atheists who are not as kindhearted. What he's alluding to is that it's the policy of Stormfront, that Christians can only recite Scripture within the Theology forums for Christians and not elsewhere in the open board. Not only that, but our CI forum is invisible to visitors and members not specifically registered for our forum. The discussion that I'm sharing with you is in the Sustaining Members forum, which is also closed to the public and allows minimal latitude for Christian dialogue, but is met with strong opposition from some quarters as you'll see.

A female pagan responds to the atheist and says, "I do not in any way believe that anyone in particular is holding back Christian Identity anymore than they are holding back any of the rest of us. As far as being selfish, let the guiltless cast the first stone (however that goes), because wanting to indulge your beliefs at the expense of everyone else strikes me as pretty darn selfish. I was responding to the 'selfish' part of your post, that I interpreted as biased against all non-CI."

That prompted me to join in the dialogue and I said, "Actually, if selfishness were the prime motivator, Christian Identity would have abandoned the languishing Titanic (a sinking ship) a long time ago, sparing ourselves a lot of intentional misrepresentations and slander. But, we have a calling to love those who hate us (and no I don't mean jews), but our own kind reject the message of hope. Another misconception is that we put religion above race [a comment that you will hear frequently in the WN movement is that their skin is their religion]. We don't put one above the other, because we consider race and faith symbiotic. One without the other is the religion of selfishness."

Mind you, I can't quote Scripture and say, *"Who changed the truth of God into a lie and worshipped and served the creature more than the Creator"* –Romans 1:25. I am forced to synthesize my thoughts into paraphrase and basic principles of the Bible. And therefore, be wise as serpents. I even say our "book" or "owner's manual", rather than the Bible so as not to offend anyone who might gripe about thumping.

When the pagan accused me of spreading my beliefs, "At the expense of everyone else", I asked, "Even if it's for the good of our race?" The pagan replied, "And by what authority does one claim to know what is good for all of us? Your God?" I could have said, "Yes, of course", but that would be like hitting a hornet's nest with a stick. So I just said, "The proof of the pudding is in the eating." What I meant by that was, the evidence that demonstrates the truth is through on-the-job training. Well, that's what lit the fuse for today's subject.

By what authority do I claim to know what is good for our entire race? I suppose what is considered 'good' is subjective. 'Winston tastes good, like a cigarette should' unless you get lung cancer. Having a chocolate sundae for breakfast, lunch and dinner 24/7 would be a good deal and a happy meal in the mind of a ten year old. A loving and caring parent might not think it's good at that rate of frequency. I can tell this pagan or any White Nationalist atheist from whence comes White Power and why it's good for them even if it's imposed upon them, contrary to their beliefs. Power is authority.

I will now quote the Word of God, not the traditions of man. From Romans 13, which only Christian Identity seems to understand, I have used the word 'authority' in lieu of other synonyms. *"Let every person submit to the governing authorities; For there is no authority except from God; the authorities that exist have been established by God. Therefore whoever resists the authority opposes what God has established; and they that resist will bring judgment on themselves. For the authorities are not a terror to good behavior, but to the evil. Would you like to live without fear of the authorities? Then do what is good and you will have praise from the same"* –Romans 13:1-3.

History is bursting at the seams with all kinds of abuse and misuse of authority for personal gain. They were to rule under God, not as if they were God themselves independent of His authority. There are at least two reasons I can think of as to why people do not do that which is good. The first is that they are ignorant of the Word, because they've never read it or second, they have read it and disagree with God.

The pagans and atheists like to mock faith and exalt science as their authority, believing that the origin of the universe was some kind of fluke or random accident and yet they have no proof. Pretty scientific huh? I Thes. 5:1 says, *"Prove all things, hold on to what is good."* Don't you think it's a good point that the very first thing the

15

Bible establishes in Gen. 1:1 is that God created the universe? Is there any other "religion" that makes that contention in the first sentence of their holy book? The non-believer would say we can't prove that, it's all just faith, as if there's something wrong with faith or that faith doesn't prove anything. Does God reckon faith as *"The evidence of things not seen"* (Heb. 11:1)? How do we secure the evidence and submit exhibits A, B, C in a court of law? You need a fully informed jury and something other than a kangaroo court and a hanging judge. Just look at who are the most vociferous opponents of Mosaic and English common law: antichrist jews, sodomites, race mixers, career criminals, corrupt politicians, thieves, liars etc. You have to wonder what authority do they think is best.

But, "Faith comes by hearing, and hearing by the Word of God." If they don't have any faith, they are deaf. How would they know what is good, if they can't hear God? How do we know what is good or what is the will of God? The simple answer is that we learn it and learn to hear His answers so that the Holy Spirit, the pure unadulterated motive of God, guides and directs us into understanding the intent of His Law and apply it according to His purposes. *"Train up a child in the way he should go; and when he is old, he will not depart from it"* –Prov. 22:6. Before he gets old, he may be rebellious, but the parent has planted the seed to learn obedience. Disobedience will always bring the guaranteed curses and accompanying judgments for sin.

In the Middle Ages, the judges in Europe would burn people at the stake or throw them in a river bound and weighted down, and if God saved them, then they were presumed innocent. In other words, God had to prove them innocent by direct divine intervention, whereas in the biblical system, God's intervention proved guilt. After the construction of the Titanic, a reporter asked the man who built it how safe it would be, and with an ironic tone he said, "Not even God can sink it."

The Protestant Reformation and the invention of the printing press made the Scriptures available so that men could study the Word. We owe our understanding of 'innocent until proven guilty' to God's Law. It's incredible that some people still judge Christianity based on the catholic church's abuse of authority, never even coming close to understanding the will of God. There's a good reason God is training Christian Identity to know good from evil, to know Jacob-Israel from Esau-Edom, to know right from wrong, to know God's authority from the authority of mortals. And that reason is to judge righteously, in godly righteousness, not to just have the authority to condemn unrighteousness, but to restore lawful order, redeeming the earth and setting matters aright by decree.

We don't always see immediate results, because when you're planting seeds, it takes time to grow; and God has all the time in the world for things to mature according to His timetable. Decrees may seem ineffectual and some people may mock them as a waste of time, but they are in operation through faith. I believe in faith healings and decrees from those endowed with the gift of healing, who are actually biblical judges, who have ruled against the disease and the wheels of death and decreed life to the sick and the dying. We are living in a dying world, we eat less and less living food, we drink fluoridated water and breathe toxic air. Our old way of thinking is sown in weakness, but the new man in Christ is raised in power (in spiritual authority).

What do we do, as lower-court judges, if we don't know the will of God in a complicated matter? Moses had the same problem with an apparent conflict of the Law, having all Israelites observing the Passover and a man touching a dead body, being unclean for seven days, and therefore couldn't come before God to keep the feast. A man had buried his father just before Passover, so Moses had to go to God because the Law hadn't dealt with such a situation before. God resolved the issue with a Supreme Court ruling in Numbers 9:10-11. The non-believers are always bringing up, 'yeah, but what about blah, blah, blah'... as if God's authority is lacking in justice or resolve.

Deut. 1:17 reassures us that there is not one problem that is too difficult for God to deal with, *"You shall not fear man, for the judgment is God's. And the case that is too hard for you, you shall bring it to Me, and I will hear it."* Problem solved. No wonder Christianity has such a bad reputation today, when so many believers are unaware of the reality of authorization to exert spiritual authority. That may explain why some people resent our beliefs "at the expense of everyone else." Real godly authority is rarely if ever seen. What is seen most commonly is the authority of self, secular humanism, the unity of the creature above the Creator;

17

just another lousy tower of Babel. See the New World Order – same as the Old World Order.

Will we ever learn? We will if we keep sowing seeds. Unfortunately, many find it difficult to comprehend biblical authority profusely exemplified throughout the Bible. These are not exceptions, but rather the rule towards a new life and a new way of thinking to come into alignment with the mind of God. To think like God does not mean that we are God. It means we have the authority to change the world around us. The non-believer does not believe we can save our race from an authority founded on faith. The mere mention of the supernatural is enough to slam the door in your face, but didn't Jesus say, "I am the door"? A closed door is a closed mind. When we enter His door, we are coming out of Babylon, the religion of selfishness. *"But a natural man* [someone who can't conceive of the supernatural and thinks God can't see them] *does not accept the things of the Spirit of God, for they are foolishness unto him; and he can't understand them, because they are spiritually discerned"* – I Cor. 2:14.

Miracles are historically progressive. Our race has gone from the phenomenon of the Old Testament to the miracles of Pentecost in the book of Acts to the present age where we will see even greater acts of the supernatural. We are not unequally yoked together with secular White Nationalists in a pretend foxhole covering each other's back waiting for Jesus to save us from the machinations of antichrist jews. No, we are here to declare victory in a spiritual warfare in the authority of Jesus Christ to claim dominion of the earth for the Kingdom of God.

Much of our spiritual training in life is designed to bring us to the predestined place of authority where we function as God's judges. And I don't mean in a black robe behind an oversized mahogany throne. The enemy would emasculate us of this divine duty and honor with the repetitious mantra of 'judge not, lest thou also be judged.' Fine with me, bring it on; show me where racism is a sin; show me where it says love the sinner, but hate the sin; show me where it says I have to submit to a ruler that is a terror to good works.

In ancient Israel, the judges were the priests and they were called to render verdicts according to the Law of God. Their decrees gave voice to the verdict, not as their own, but as the judgment of God (Deut. 1:17). The Word says the men of Israel have been made kings and priests (Ex. 19:6; Rev. 5:10), a kingdom of priests, because we serve the King of kings and judge all things according to His Law. Men can decree things till they're blue in the face, but if their authority is not in accord with the mind of Christ led by the Spirit, their decrees are curses upon the land. Want a White Nationalist movement led by godless men? Curses! Want a black communist ruling over you? Curses! Want any other authority than God? Curses! To know the mentality of separating righteousness from unrighteousness is a matter of life and death for any White community or nation who are called by God to exercise spiritual authority in any area of society.

We used to have a member in our church back in Washington who would request prayer for Morris Dees to die in a fiery car crash. Obviously, this did not happen, although the prayers have never been rescinded, because one cannot decree successfully unless it is an earthly expression of the divine will and plan and in the Lord's timing. It's not enough to know the will of God. One must also know when to implement it. Timing is important, because time is the link between the will and the plan. Years ago we prayed against Benny Hinn at one of his dog and pony shows. Just recently, his wife filed for divorce. That doesn't say much for what some of his followers call "the anointed of God." It takes time to bring down the Nimrods.

I caught a segment on MSNBC (2/23/11) where the SPLC reported that in 2011, the number of hate groups is now over 1000, a new record. This means that there is a growing number of White people who hate the authority that is being imposed upon them. Well, what do you expect when a society allows a group like the SPLC to be an authority on hate? My authority is Proverbs 8:13, *"Fear of the Lord is to hate evil."*

The SPLC has no fear of godly authority, because it loves to defend evil. This is what I would call an accident waiting to happen and a little prayer of encouragement just may hasten the day of God's wrath. When a society rejects the authority of God, can you really expect blessings upon our race? Let's read Hosea 9:17, *"My God will cast them away, because they did not hearken unto Him; and they shall be wanderers among the nations."* At first glance, one thinks of the wandering jew. However, it's the true Israel (found in the

19

White race) that has been whoring after strange gods, looking in all the wrong places for an authority to give them a good life. *"When the righteous are in authority, the people rejoice; but when the wicked rule, the people mourn"* – Prov. 29:2.

The secular authority of jewish thinking permeates just about everything in American society except Christian Identity. It's this Hindu creed of a million gods that says, "One shall not condemn another religion or race by word or deed" that has infected the mentality of White Nationalism; at the expense of its own survival that strikes me as suicidal. It has happened already with the judeo-Christian churches being contaminated with universalism. If a White Nationalist leader says they are not a White Supremacist, it can only mean one of two things: they are either equal to the other races or they are inferior. My Bible says, *"The Lord thy God hath chosen thee... to be above all people that are upon the face of the earth"* – Deut. 7:6. We are warned that there is a very real possibility that the enemies of our race "shall become the head, and we shall become the tail" if we do not hearken and observe God's authority (Deut. 28:13, 44).

It is the will of God that His chosen race takes dominion of the whole earth and that all things should be "under His feet." However, as Paul writes in Hebrews 2:8, *"we do not yet see all things put under Him."* Indeed, we are put to shame when savage beasts of the jungle become the head and we become the brainless tail; when mamzers brown the complexion of our posterity and blackens our sense of morality. Why don't some of our people have eyes to see it? It's because our race has been judicially blinded. *"As it is written [Isa. 29:10], God has given the spirit of slumber, eyes that they should not see, and ears that they should not hear; unto this day"* – Romans 11:9.

And then we read in verse 25, *"Blinded in part is happened to Israel, until the fullness of the Gentiles be come in."* The KJV is sometimes very hard to understand, because it's so poorly translated, but the key word here is "until", suggesting that everybody will eventually see what Christian Identity sees. I think the Ferrar Fenton version gives us a partial clue by translating 'Gentiles' as 'heathen'; in other words, the non-White peoples of the earth. Because of a greatly misappropriated application of the 'Great Commission' and the universalism of catholic/jewish/hindu evangelists, the racially mixed multitudes have come into our land and just look at the churches full of strangers. The judeo-Christian evangelists have provided for the fullness of the racial alien's belly to come in and devour our land.

"Who is blind, but My servant? Or deaf, as My messenger that I sent? Who is blind as he that is perfect [racially pure] and blind as the Lord's servant?... Who among you will give ear to this? Who will hearken and hear for the time to come?" What time? A time of a much needed deliverance. An alien heathen cannot comprehend the authority of God, because God never intended for them to have it. So what authority has superseded God's Law? It's the authority of strangers and their strange gods. "Who gave Jacob for a spoil, and Israel to the robbers? Did not the Lord, He against whom we have sinned? For they would not walk in His ways, neither were they obedient unto His Law" – Isaiah 42:24 (and the above verses 23 and 19 respectively).

Do you think Paul wanted his brethren to be ignorant of this mystery, Mystery Babylon, a religious system of rampant race mixing and perversions, to be wise in our own conceited mutation of authority? No, he was heralding the day that our people would awaken from their slumber and be wise with the vision that there is no power or authority but of God. Are you going to serve the God of segregation or the gods of integration? We are the part of Israel that isn't blind and we are obligated, as disciples of Christ to plant the seeds of hope and that His Law is not grievous.

Hear the truth of Christ, "For My yoke is easy and My burden is light" – Mt. 11:30. When our race sees that there is only one authority, it says we'll be saved (Romans 11:26). Jesus said to Israel only, *"Come unto Me, all ye that labor and are heavy laden, and I will give you rest"* (Mt. 11:28). Lord knows, we need a rest from years of the rising tide of color and colorable law as it was in the days of Noah and Lot. Our kindred will be awakened by the overcomers, the saints, the Remnant of Israel that did not bend the knee to alien authorities.

As aliens come in, we are commanded to come out, that we might not receive the plagues. That door of Christ might be more of an exit than an entrance. 'That we should show forth the praises of Him who has called us out of darkness and into His marvelous light" I

Peter 2:9. Being God's judge is a commission, a way of life. It is the supernatural consequences of being led by the Spirit and having enough faith for you and others as well. The ultimate goal is to make 'Thy will be done, on earth as it is in heaven' the reality, establishing the authority of Christ throughout the whole world, which is His after all.

Our brethren cannot continue to wander in the dark, not able to find their way, without the Light of the world. Jesus Christ has the divine right of kings to rule the world. Others deny Him and advocate democracy or the rule of the mob, as we see going on in many Arab countries today, which usually has the hidden hand of evil lurking in the shadows. Strangers and strange gods flock into America and the bitter fruit of secular humanism is almost ripe. God usually waits until the fruit can be tasted and known for what it is before cutting it down and burning it. Some of us can see the end of an age and the start of a new one. We stand at the crossroads where the glory of God will grind the guilty to powder. If you know what to look for, the stone of Daniel 2:35 is bringing down the image of Babylon. *"And in the days of those kings the God of heaven will set up a kingdom which will never be destroyed, and that kingdom will not be left for another people; it will crush and put an end to all these kingdoms, but it will itself endure forever"* – Daniel 2:44.

This is the Kingdom of Heaven, symbolized by a stone, a stone which the builders rejected. But the Kingdom will start with little ecclesias like God's Fellowship of Covenant People and grow from there to a confederation of fellowships wanting to be ruled by Jesus Christ. The Kingdom will have one King and one authority for all White Christians. The blessings that God showers upon His people will cause all Israelite nations to flow unto the house of the Lord (Is. 2:2). Jesus said there would be "outer darkness" (maybe something like a Detroit in Uganda) where people would dwell outside the Kingdom of Light, where they could enjoy the fruits of their secular authorities.

In the coming age, all the failures of Israel and the church will be corrected by perfect leadership – by righteous overcomers who know God's Laws and the intent of those Laws. The Kingdom will not have perfect citizens, but they will all be believers who will conform to the righteous authority of God as they are led by the

Spirit. As long as the Stone continues to grind, we will have some rough days ahead, but they will be exciting days if you have eyes to see. The good news is that the grinding process is designed to set the earth free from the corruption of secular governments and leaders that have no business leading. The false prophets having the planet going up in smoke will be proven wrong.

The world and our race are being given the opportunity to be redeemed by their Kinsman Redeemer. This message is a calling to the hardened hearts, the losers and the lost to come out of the dark side of your minds and walk through the door to the winning side. May our Lord make His face shine upon them and be gracious for the scales to fall from their eyes. God said He would put His authority upon the children of Israel and bless them. Let us be worthy recipients and lead the unworthy to unmerited favor with God. But for the grace of God, there go I.

Chapter 2

Our History - His Story

From the beginning of Adamic Creation, the pendulum of time has swung back and forth between the secular independence of our racial identity and a commitment to the divine origin of our race. A dependence upon the latter is what Christian Identity has rediscovered. Our race has been riddled with foreign concepts over the millennia challenging the idea that our race is an inextricable component of the God of Creation and God, as evidenced in His Word, has a blueprint of predestination for us.

As a people, we seem to drift in and out of the cognitive response to the supernatural realities of why we exist. The appellation of 'God's chosen people' has been obfuscated by conspiracy and manipulation of the pendulum, which denies the preeminence of White Christian civilization. Indeed, the preponderance of propaganda conjures an image of Jesus Christ as being a jew to the average misnomered gentile.

In fact, we are hounded and ridiculed at the slightest suggestion of White Supremacy or the truth about ancient Israel as it relates to us today. The Identity message is a constant story of a race of people being lost and found. Christ came for the "lost sheep" (Mt. 15:24) and promised them that if they would seek after something, they would find it (Mt. 7:7).

In this day and age there is an "increase in knowledge", albeit a plethora of disinformation in the mix designed to deceive us. However, the truth is out there for discerning explorers. It is difficult for people to accept that their beloved leaders have lied to them. And yet 50 years after Pearl Harbor, we find FDR had prior knowledge of the attack. Even more oblique and underhanded is the unscrupulous scholar who chronicles past events to accommodate a given power structure or ruling system. This practice, of course, colors and taints the innocent student from learning. The old adage 'to the victors of war go the spoils', which would include the license to posture their own historical record, could also be applied to the politics of translating the Bible.

Would anyone dare interpolate the Word of God? When corruption rules the day, this becomes a very real probability. The Bible warns us of 'another gospel' and 'false teachers'. Our enemies don't want us to know our heritage, the rock from whence we were hewn, and are therefore destroying the evidence and memories of who we really are. The realization that our people are blind to their Adamic/Israelite identity is nothing new. There's nothing new under the sun for a reason. *"Blindness in part is happened to Israel"* (Romans 11:25).

Hosea 1:10 declared our kin of old, before Christ, to have lost and found their identity, just as it shall be said of us today, that 'ye are not My people' until you understand who you are: 'ye are the sons of the living God'. There are so many ways in which our race can be estranged from God, but the primary cause is adultery or mongrelization. That is to say 'whoring after strange gods', which can only be accomplished by associating with strangers/other races. We lose our identity when we adapt to other cultures and their mores.

Unfortunately, the religion of the West has become an adulterated oxymoron known as judeo-Christianity. It is an unholy blend of Hinduism, Mithra, Zoroaster, Baal worship and Judaism just to name a few of the culprits. The challenge before Christian Identity is to expunge these commonly accepted abominations of theological sophistries and restore our biblical heritage.

The first century apostolic church was an Identity movement, in that the disciples were reaching out with the good news gospels to their own kind. The message was not preached to non-Whites, because the Great Commission did not include them. When Israel went into Assyrian captivity she lost sight of who she was. These tribes, whom Josephus describes as an 'inestimable number', corresponds to British historian Sharon Turner tracing our race back to this very territory. They moved westward across Europe, under different names, but remained the same racial stock of Israelites, becoming the Anglo-Saxon-Celtic peoples, whom history testifies as the willing recipients of primitive Christianity.

The putative misperception that the Catholic church of Rome was the cradle of Christianity betrays the truth that our Israelitish faith was planted in the British Isles within a very few years after the Crucifixion. The beast of Catholicism was a means to eclipse the Identity message to the White race and vicariously assume the authority of Christ's church with its adulterated polar opposite of incorporating the strange gods of non-Israelite cultures into the amalgamated bipolar universal religions we see today. We see a lot of its priesthood to be comprised of sodomites and pedophiles with bishops complacent to its perverse presence.

The devils (rabbis) of Judaism also work in consort with the false church to establish a stronghold of antichrist diversity; thereby preempting the Kingdom of God and the idea that White people will ever know who they really are. Just to show you that the premise of Christian Identity is not exactly a recent phenomenon, all the student has to do is ascertain whether or not bona fide history confirms or denies that White people have known and believed that they are the true Israelites of the Bible.

It is not the point of this treatise to prove our ancestry. Many fine Christian Identity researchers have already established our historical link to ancient Israel. What needs to be examined and analyzed is the modern revival of this wonderful truth.

The Scottish Declaration of Independence of 1320 AD makes the connection between Scotland and Israel of old an immutable fact.

The Scots did not consider this controversial. However, Scotland was not as compromised as England to the south, when they (the British) soon came to the pernicious usurers of the Talmud, eager to prove the root of all evil. The progression of Christian Identity came to England in 1649 with a barnacle of subterfuge. But the precursor before that, the road to building the empire was paved by the notorious King Henry VIII and his seizure of the Church of England after he defied the Vatican. Geopolitical war quickly became spiritual warfare of religious ideas and concepts between the Pope and the Monarchy.

John Dee (1527-1608), the son of a court official during Henry's reign, grew up surrounded by this conflict and the mystical currents transforming an impoverished little island into a powerful empire. One of the best kept secrets of English history is that Dee was not only the grand architect of the British empire itself, being the chief consul and advisor to the Protestant Queen Elizabeth, but also the satanic occult founder of Freemasonry, while introducing Rosicrucianism to Germany.

To forge alliances between jewish money and British imperialism, John Dee developed a common racial identity between the two with the concept of British-Israel, invoking biblical prophecy to justify their world takeover. This was nothing less than an intelligence coup carried out by occult propaganda. However, this act of treachery should never be confused with the truth itself. Oftentimes exploitation cannot succeed without the credibility of a truth distracting us from the thin veneer of deceit. All this set the stage for the later absorption of European jewry into British society and the corrupted definition of Israel. The new royal jews became masters of fraud. That great fraud perpetrated was not the money itself, but rather the jewish obsession to monopolize every penny for themselves.

After Edward I expelled the jews in 1290, England enjoyed economic prosperity and stability for over 300 years. All of Europe followed their lead with purging the jews from their land. But the conniving jews bided their time to return to the easy pickings of Christian nations. As we'll see, a more sinister plot for a one-world order run by jews was being schemed. For the jew, true Christianity and the White race stood in their way. What happened in 1649, after the beheading of Charles I, was a secret meeting between Oliver

27

Cromwell and Rabbi Manasseh ben Israel of Holland to allow jews to return to England in return for money.

The religious canard for allowing the readmission of jews into England was the reunification of all the tribes of Israel. This constituted the Europeans nations, including the house of Judah, which the jews falsely claimed to be. With this impersonation, the jews said the second advent of Christ could be fulfilled. With this new found relationship and money, Cromwell could pursue his fratricidal wars against Ireland and Scotland as well as crushing a large number of Christian churches and monasteries (including Glastonbury) confiscating the church properties and treasuries, splitting the loot with his new jewish cronies. The historical record now reveals that with this traitorous agreement, titles of nobility would be issued to wealthy jews, ushering in the Bank of England (1694) and a corrupt Church of England.

It is ironic that the negotiations for the Bank were conducted in a church. With this illegitimate marriage of the truth and a lie, Britain and jewry, came the blessings and curses of a colonial empire. Together, they would rule the world. Techniques of political power used in times past paled in comparison to the new system of a ruthless oligarchy, which the jews had penetrated with their usurious money. This was an important pivotal time in history where great forward strides were being made in the matrimony of international jewish finance and the English aristocracy, which has materially and spiritually changed the way of life today for nearly every person on the face of the earth.

It can be shown that John's Revelation of modern Mystery Babylon of economic/religious transformation started in earnest in England at the time of Cromwell. The dissolution of traditional Christian churches supplanted with a new judaized version was the necessary gamble that jews had to wage for their new world order i.e. a Pax Judaica.

Part of this enticement was the idea of who God's chosen people were. To this day, there are jewish organizations such as the United Israel World Union, who freely admit that the Anglo-Saxon-Celtic peoples are the lost sheep of the house of Israel with themselves as the long lost brethren of Judah of course. They also despise Christian Identity for exposing their false identity as Judah and so, out of necessity, have gone to great lengths to demonize the Christian Identity movement. Ironically, they are the epitome of demonic and satanic personas (rather than their contrived mythology of a so called "Satan" or demons to distract "goyim" from themselves), which have used secret societies and the Talmudic occult to control the world with a total disregard for human life.

The impact of this phenomenon is that the peoples of the world have surreptiously succumbed to the satanic influence of jews. Even Christian Identity has been victimized in this regard in the form of certain doctrines. Once the jews gained a foothold in the body politic of England, more perverse adulterations of who God's chosen people were could mutate into a spiritualized Israel with jews assuming the helm of governments.

From the time of Cromwell to the time of Dr. Samuel Maitland and John Darby, the Christian identity of White people became blurred, thanks to the apostate teaching of the Rapture, which was predicated on the lie of jewish people returning as Israelites to their homeland in Palestine before the second coming of Christ could occur. Being that those who call themselves jews today have no claim to the namesake of Judah, it is pure chutzpah to say it is their home.

Having said all this, in order to present a history of Christian Identity, the only theology closely resembling true Christianity was a remnant of believers that adhered to the understanding of who the Israel people of the Bible were. It was called British Israel and it is still around today. Unfortunately, back then, perhaps out of gratitude for being reminded as to whom they were, the English allowed the idea of jews being Judah to remain uncontested. The jews never could have pulled off their religious/political/economic scam by themselves.

Before the BBC and the technological revolution of mass brainwashing, Englishmen entertained themselves with titillating eccentricities and peculiar intellectual parlor games. After Cromwell's destruction of the traditional Christian church and ethic, the Church of England manipulated a politically correct ecclesiastical establishment directing what later in history became known as the judeo-Christian ethic. Although the jews reentered England on the premise that Anglo-Saxondom was the lost tribes of

Israel, the premise was soon diluted to a spiritualized 'New Israel' rather than the physical racial descendants.

Bubbles of truth would occasionally float to the surface of the public's consciousness. However, the Trojan horse of jewry attached itself to a variety of growing interests related to the Bible like a parasite on a host body. One such independent formation of theology away from the establishment church was the British Israel movement, which was more than just an idea; while attracting followers to the writings of John Wilson appearing in 1815 to his death in 1871.

Wilson's lectures found a large middle class audience in Ireland and England. The pieces of the puzzle began fitting together as it was shown that many social institutions were the result of an Israelite legacy influenced by the migrating tribes across the nations of Europe. It was a diaspora that reflected the ancient righteousness of everything that was moral and British. But then enters the pernicious jew, which Wilson knew did not fit into the picture. He was skeptical of jewish claims of Old Testament ancestry, maintaining that descendants of Judah, having patterns of miscegenation, were now an inferior race cursed with mongrelization. The fly in his ointment however, was the misguided notion that the curse could be broken by accepting Jesus as the Son of God. The antichrist jews, thus, enjoyed the easy pickings of fraternal tolerance and a liberal minded patronization to interact in the state of affairs of England.

Wilson could appreciate other nations of Europe as tribal kindred, especially the Teutonic history of Germany, which we have identified today as the true tribe of Judah. This would be a curious point of contention, for later proponents of the British Israel movement, not willing to share their divine destiny with non-English peoples. The imperial British expansionism of colonial rule fueled concepts of manifest destiny i.e. the Christian mandate to take dominion of the earth. This of course has led to innumerable debates over claims of racial supremacy or the converse ideology of racial equality. The latter contention was interestingly enough, the brainchild of Karl Marx and other jewish communists having worldly ambitions. It was just as important to these rabbinic intellectuals to keep a lid on the British Israel movement then, as it is to neutralize the Christian Identity movement now.

After Wilson's death, Edward Hine assumed leadership of a more exclusive, consolidated promulgation of Anglo-centric doctrine, revising Wilson's friendly position towards Germany into disfavor. As God was prospering a thriving industrial Germany, a jealous English public increasingly became suspicious of their European brethren and so began priming the future for world wars of fratricide. Naturally, the jews encouraged and harbored this hatred for the German people. Hine misidentified Germany as a modern day Assyria and elevated jews as a part of Israel and hence, must come together as a matter of eschatology, hinting at the resettlement of Palestine, which would later materialize in the Balfour Declaration in 1917, making it the "too often promised land."

Despite British Israel's popularity, the movement never organized as an effective body politic. Its adherents were not required to disenfranchise themselves with establishment denominations. As a consequence, there was no authority to screen false doctrines engrafted onto British Israel theology. Christian Identity has a similar problem today with people bringing in denominational baggage into the movement.

Hine attempted to create his own organization in 1873 called the British-Israel Corporation, but it failed. It would seem that God allows disinformation for a season. *"It is the glory of God to conceal a thing, but the honor of kings is to search out a matter"* −Prov. 25:2. Christ hath made us kings (Rev. 1:6) and is "Kings of kings" and they that are with Him are called and chosen. Identity is the perfect word for our calling today, but infections riddle its divine destiny. Deviating from God's Word infects the integrity of the message and the movement. Let us learn from the imperfections of leadership of times past. It is our history and His Story. The irony of the British Israel movement was a conspiracy of jews, race traitors and the Church of England gambling on the revelation of a truth for political gain, whereby adherents of British Israel predominantly remain in the state church.

On the other hand, divine providence could not exclude America from British Israel's special relationship between Ephraim and Manasseh in Bible prophecy. We can therefore witness the progression of our true manifest destiny as White people naturally

31

gravitate towards the racial truth that shall make us free. Christian Identity has evolved from the British Israel movement and has been growing for over 50 years. May the God of Israel continue to distil in His people an unfolding story of our calling that will only magnify His glory.

Chapter 3

The Real Armageddon

This title is a play on words from an old TV game show of the 1960's, To Tell The Truth. The celebrity panelists would try to guess which one of the three contestants were not lying. After questions and answers, the host of the show would ask the real Mr. so and so to please stand up. The bona fide truth teller would rise and the audience would erupt with applause. Today, we see the truth taking a terrible pounding. The treatise of this book is to resuscitate the fight for that which will set us free from the bondage of lies. May the real Armageddon, God willing, rise up and tower over the plethora of falsehoods.

Perhaps one of the greatest tragedies of this century is the power to change the meaning of words, whereby definitions slip away into an insidious memory hole, after the manner of George Orwell's 1984 (totalitarian mind control). The tragedy is that an entire race, the White race, is being led into slavery and slaughter by the gradual erosion of language. The control of hearts and minds is manifest in an opposite direction of what God intends. The sub-human usurpers will craftily call evil good and good evil. This we can plainly see in our midst today with the legitimization of immoral behavior that in times past would have been punishable by death. There are masters of deceit that stretch generations to accomplish their sinister ulterior motives. Their goal is world dominion and manipulating communications is an integral part of their conspiratorial intrigues. Therefore, it is imperative to examine these words that have been incredulously foisted upon us in a most damaging hoax; that with the lift of God's Word we will expose its dark and evil fraud.

That most significant word is Armageddon. Let us proceed to dissect the cancer from the truth and may God's mercy lift the fog of confusion, so that those with eyes may see and understand. The purpose of this treatise is to remove the barnacles from the trumpets of deliverance and proclaim liberty throughout the land. Let freedom loving Christians shake off the shackles of lies and put on the whole armor of our God given racial heritage.

Definition of Armageddon

Revelation 16:16 is the only place in the Bible where this word, Armageddon, appears. We find from Strong's Concordance that this Greek word [1] means a symbol and is derived from two Hebrew words: Har [2], meaning a mountain or range of hills sometimes used figuratively as a country and, Megiddon [3], meaning a rendezvous [4]. Webster's Seventh New Collegiate Dictionary defines rendezvous as a place appointed for assembling and symbol as a creedal form, a visible sign of something invisible. Some ministers denounce the use of a concordance so that they may keep their flocks in darkness, similar to possession of God's Word being forbidden to the people prior to the Protestant Reformation. The common denominator that forms the Christian creed (or belief), contrary to what false teachers may say, throughout the entire Bible, is the physical role of Israel, for whom God selected to receive His Word [5]. The Bible is addressed to this race of people only; all others are incidental as they may interrelate to Israel. Interestingly, the book of Revelation, a vision of St. John, is predominantly symbolic, so we must observe II Timothy 2:15 in studying and properly understanding what is written, because it is either for our good or detriment as to how these interpretations are applied to our lives.

Unfortunately, the real context of Revelation 16:16 has been ignored and falsely exploited to rob White Christians economically, for a bandit political state in Tel Aviv, in the form of foreign aid via federal income taxes. The tactics of the Israeli Lobby are intense. To the criminal mind it makes sense to bribe American officials in the various branches of government, if the return is a thousand fold or more to their advantage. There are antichrists such as Zionists, Talmudic Jews, socialists/communists and Judeo-Christian traitors who would fall flat on their face if it were not for the belief system that promulgates the false teaching that Armageddon is associated with a battle in the Middle East. The key to our study is location and the identification of the people involved. It is intellectual dishonesty to say that Armageddon is a battle or valley. The claims of the Israeli Jews based on Biblical extrapolation and fabricated conjecture cannot be proven upon a close investigation. In fact, upon scrutiny of their contentions, no theological or historical evidence can honestly lend support. Armageddon has to do with the Israel people, but not to the imposters that steal the birthright today.

As we shall see, *Israel* is not synonymous with 'Jew'; never has been and never will be. People often perceive what they think to be the truth as a result of what they hear first or is most repeated and corresponds to their own personal notions of what truth is. And truth usually suffers as being accepted last. Many seek an easier, softer way but truth is not mocked. The blood of the saints and martyrs of Christendom have not preserved the eternal principles of God in vain. Nor will today's patriots tolerate compromise. We are approaching an ultimate conflagration between good and evil. No one will escape choosing which side he/she will serve. However, the term 'battle of Armageddon' is not to be found anywhere in the Bible! These references to that great battle are more correctly called 'the day of the Lord'; when the proud and lofty tares of Mystery Babylon, a system of corruption, are purged and cleansed for the incoming Kingdom of Christ on earth [6]. It is not a nuclear blast vaporizing the planet, but rather the dissolving of ungodly elements that will not enter the Kingdom [7].

Armageddon or the gathering is not the battle itself, but is associated with the prophecies of the destruction of God's enemies. These enemies of Christ, the self-appointed chosen ones, fear the truth of the gathering and most assuredly are working towards the prevention of the true Armageddon. God cannot be stopped and White Christians need not fear the inevitable. In Revelation 16:18 a great earthquake follows the gathering of verse 16. If this is not a literal earthquake, could it be something else that shook the world, something like World War I and II? Yes! Remember, this is a vision.

If you are a Christian, it is your duty and reward to dig up the hidden treasures of God. Jesus spoke in parables because the mysteries of His Kingdom (government) were given only to a specific people and denied to others [8]. It is the glory of God to conceal a thing, but the honor of kings is to search out a matter [9]. Your attitude will determine whether or not the truth be revealed. If your heart is waxed gross and you give reverence to the status quo of the world, then that which you obey and follow will be your god [10]. Choose you this day whom ye will serve [11]. Realize that there are two kinds of pain: 1. Discipline weighing ounces and 2. Regret weighing tons. Chapters 17 and 18 of Revelation describe the subsequent judgment and destruction upon Mystery Babylon. Armageddon or the gathering precedes the fall of God's enemies and we are to rejoice over her [12] as those who subscribed to the hoax weep [13].

Linguistics experts say there is a striking similarity to the Hebrew and English language. In Zephaniah 3:9 after pouring out of the Lord's wrath upon the earth, the Lord will instill a pure language for universal service. The only proven element of unity in God's good purpose is English, which is synonymous with the White race, who are heirs of the promises given to ancient Israel. Then in verse 20, in no uncertain terms, God blesses the same race of people with a name and praise among all the races. The genealogies of Jesus are given because of the importance God places on racial bloodlines. Do not make the mistake of spiritualizing away that which God has foreordained. To clearly decipher the vision of Revelation 16:16 let us rephrase it thus: "And he gathered the tribes (nations) of Israel (the White race) together into a place called, in English, the united states of America." The name *America* comes from the word 'Ameri' meaning heavenly, and 'rica' meaning kingdom, hence the heavenly kingdom.

Chapter 4

The Racial Identification
of Israel

There are three views entertained by Christians as to who the Israel people of the Holy Bible are, namely: 1. The church, 2. The Jews, and 3. The Anglo Saxon and kindred people. It behooves all serious inquiries to let the scriptures establish the answer. For too long, the first two nominees have virtually gone uncontested and now that they are being challenged, the burden of proof is found wanting. The third group claiming identity as Israel is the most controversial and has been forced to scholastically produce the evidence (it is not based on the say-so of their pastors).

Therefore, what sayeth God's Word? Jesus announced to the Jews (followers and leaders of the Babylonian Talmud), who had rejected Him in Matthew 21:43, that the Kingdom shall be taken from you (Jews) and given to a nation (Israel). When has the church ever been a nation? Never! Some suggest that Israel is now spiritualized. Considering all scriptures on the subject, this would make God a liar, contradicting all the references made about it. And Romans 11:29 says the gifts and calling of God are not subject to change.

If any book can be called a racial book, it is the Bible. The same chosen people continue and remain chosen. Galatians 3:16 points to this fact. God does not advocate pluralism or a national blessing upon a melting pot of races (seeds). The Holy command for racial separation is discussed in a later chapter of this study. To eliminate race is a grave injustice and denial of what God has created for His purposes. Amalgamation and integration are self-serving non Christian concepts. These ideologies cannot coexist with God's Word. That is why the meaning of scriptures must be changed – to serve their purposes (not God's). If you don't want race rightly discerned, then you really don't want God in your life. Your god is from the vain imaginations of the destroyers of race.

God's chosen people are specifically by blood inheritance. Abraham had many sons, but the inheritance was to descend through only one. The son is identified in Genesis 21:12 and Romans 9:7 for in Isaac shall thy seed (race) be called. Seed is genetic, not something sentimentally wished for or spiritualized. Indeed, the name of Anglo Saxons derives from Isaac's sons. The covenant God made with Abraham was confirmed to Isaac in Genesis 26:3-5 to make thy seed/race to multiply as the stars of heaven and giving them countries in which all the nations of the earth will be blessed. Genesis 17:4-7 tells us of an everlasting covenant with Abraham, that thou shalt be a father of many nations and that these blessings would be passed along to future generations of the same racial lineage. Psalm 105:6-10 commands the same for a thousand generations (40,000 years). Jacob passed along the covenant blessings to Joseph's sons; Genesis 48:19 says Manasseh shall be great, but the younger brother Ephraim shall be greater, his seed shall become a multitude of nations. If you compare the history of Jews in contradistinction to Anglo Saxons, regarding these promises, it should become readily apparent as to who is fulfilling the role of the prophetic heirs.

At this point, it should be obvious that the church cannot be a candidate assuming the title of Israel. The church today is not the same biblical entity of 2000 years ago. It has become the apostate organ and propaganda mill of 501c3 state sanctioned ecclesiastical thought police. These congregations are Baal-centered and if Christ returned to them in the flesh and told them their doctrines were from the pits of darkness, they would try to crucify Him again. Ye

38

shall know them by their fruits. If the Judeo-Christian ministers upheld God's laws, statutes and judgment and made sure the people heard and obeyed them, then the people would not have tolerated corruption and evil that permeates society [14].

The Greek word for church is *ekklesia* and means 'a calling out' or the leaders advocating a new way of living subservient to Jesus Christ not Caesar or the Federal government. Today's mutant churches are the whited sepulchers unequally yoked together with darkness. We need a calling out to be separate from unrighteousness, from learning the way of the heathen. The true Christian church survives without the architecture of Freemasonry or synagogues of satanic Jews. In Deuteronomy 7:6, Israel is chosen above all other races of people in the earth. This prompts the question of racial superiority and whether or not White Supremacy is scriptural. See Appendix A for a closer examination of this label.

Remember that God has His reasons for choosing things the way He does. Ironically, the name Manasseh means forgetful. The most poignant trait of Israel is its blindness as to who it is. Who is blind but the Lord's servant race and messengers and His witnesses of the Old Testament [15]? And who has blindness to their identity and responsibilities happened to in the New Testament but Israel [16]?

Most Judaized Christians are blind to the distinctions between the Assyrian and Babylonian captivities or the subsequent movements of the northern (Israel) and southern (Judah) tribes. Jesus was not referring to the 42,360 of Judah [17], returning from the Babylonian captivities in 536 B.C. to Jerusalem in Matthew 15:24 but rather He said, *"I am not sent but unto the lost sheep of the house of Israel"* (the 10 tribes of the northern house). These millions of Israelites were lost because over the centuries of geographical dislocation, their Hebrew language, religion and heritage evaporated.

This is not to be confused with racial assimilation, as history records the genetic integrity of their westward migrations into Europe. The Europeans did not suddenly appear out of thin air shortly after the end of the Assyrian captivity. Is it coincidence that the Caucasus mountains are just north of the Assyrian territories with people known as Caucasians? The Great Commission of the apostles was to go to their racial kinsmen and awaken them to the good news of the gospels. These lost sheep of His flock would be receptive and would

39

hear the message of Jesus, whereas non-Israelites would not believe upon the Lord [18]. The disciples did not trek into the jungles of Africa or slop through Oriental rice paddies. They went to their White brethrn in Judea first and then later along the northern shores of the Mediterranean, from Turkey to Spain and into France and Britain (the isles). With the advent of Christ, it is foretold that His people would have a name change.

Let's untangle the confusion of the word-manipulators by reading Isaiah 65:15, And ye shall leave your name (Jew) for a curse (Revelation 2:9 the blasphemy of them [Pharisees] which say they are Jews [Judahites] and are not; as are today's Jews falsely claiming to be God's chosen) unto my chosen (Israelites): for the Lord God shall slay thee (the destruction of Jerusalem in 70 A.D.) and call His servants (Israel) by another name. And in Isaiah 62:2 the Gentiles (those Israelites dispersed from the Assyrian captivity and scattered abroad, James 1;1) shall see thy righteousness... and thou shalt be called a new name: which is Christian (Acts 11:26). In Hosea 1:10-11 Israel's identity is lost and found in divorcement with God and future restoration; we are the sons of the living God and we have been gathered together into Christian nations. Make sense?

God is not the author of confusion and leaves us clues to identify His people throughout the ages with an important sign. That sign is the observation and keeping of the sabbath [19]. There is only one group of people that have fulfilled this sign perpetually: the White Christian Israelites. We can further fingerprint the people of Armageddon by listing the identification marks God has placed upon them. No amount of evidence will convince a hard-core atheist about the existence of God nor the following proofs persuade those of vested interests in the error of their Judaized doctrines. My prayer is that each block of information can be pieced together so that the chief cornerstone may be rightly placed upon it. This then is the foundation that Jesus Christ is glorified. See Appendix B.

Chapter 5

The Blessings of Israel

No other race of people have been blessed or can compare with Anglo Saxon Israel. The Jews have lived in ghettos like parasites on a host (nation) and rightly expelled because of their repugnant religious practices (occultism, sexual perversions, ritual murders, criminal business ethics et cetera). Their psychotic persecution complex would hardly admit their sordid history as being blessed. The Negro is only a few centuries removed from the jungle and still exhibits wild reactions outside of their natural environment and culture, due to limited intelligence and creativity; they are a frustrated race out of their element. The Oriental is subjected to an anthill of poverty and disease where ignorance and fears abound. All other ethnic minorities are complaining about their miserable lot in life for one reason or another. But the history of the White man rises above all others. Only a blind fool would deny the White Christian race is responsible for the advancement of civilization. And of course nothing happens without the guiding hand of Almighty God.

Even the divine chastisements of our people are a blessing in disguise as we shall see in Chapter 7. We can trace the initial blessing back to Abraham in Genesis 22:16 because he obeyed the Lord. Jacob's dream of Genesis 28:12-15 has the Lord giving him land, with a progeny that will spread abroad (v.14) and returning to the land (v.15 fulfilled by Israel coming out of Egypt). The birthright promises of material prosperity given to Jacob and his seed were national in scope and without conditions. There was also the promise of Genesis 49:10 that the sceptre shall not depart from Judah (they would be the custodians of the kingly throne) until Christ the messiah (king and high priest) shall the gathering (Armageddon) of the people be.

The spiritual blessings of Christ's first advent brought grace (divine influence upon the heart, unmerited gift) with the condition of faith as the faith of Abraham was (when he obeyed and God blessed him and his offspring) so that the promise is assured to our race; Romans 4:16-17 a father of many nations (there are numerous White nations). The second advent of Christ will assume the throne of David here on earth [20] where He takes the sceptre to reign over Israel. Do not confuse this with His heavenly throne where He sits now. Nowhere in the scriptures will you find the scepter or Israel in heaven, the abode of God [21].

We (a remnant of Israel) are elected by God in Romans 11:5. It is a spiritually minded Israel within national Israel. God is not electing non-Israelites (v. 1), it is only by grace that we see who we are and what God wants us to do, while the rest of Israel is blinded (v.7). The blessing for His elect in Israel is that Armageddon will transpire as we do our duty in declaring Christ as the head of government [22]. Rejection of corruption in high places of government and secular humanism in our communities will fade away (v.35). The new heaven and new earth is a Christian society in which we live – not in outer space.

To find out how blessings work with God turn to Genesis 12:2-3. God blesses the nation of Israel, making its name great [23] and says that it will be a blessing; God will bless them that bless us and curse them that curse us and in our White race shall all the other races of the earth be blessed. America has not been blessed as blinded Americans have supported the Israeli Jews; since 1948 we have been going downhill with curses. Don't you think it makes sense to quit blessing the Jesus killers? II Chronicles 19:2 says, wrath is upon us if we help or love those who hate the Lord.

It's sad [24] that our racial kinsmen in Israel (v.3) are so ignorant about God adopting us as His sons for the glory, the covenants, giving of the law, service of God and the promises (v.4), that belonged to our racial forefathers and is why Christ came concerning the flesh (the genetic heirs). Psalms 78:5-6 commands the fathers in Israel to make God's laws known to their posterity. Only Israel has been given God's Word; no other race is relevant regarding what God has decided in this matter [25]. The New Covenant is made with Israel only [26]. We are made different because He supernaturally put His law into our mind and written in our hearts, as He has not done with any other people.

And so, God wants His people to dwell alone [27]; to be separate. God made the separation and distinction, not man [28]. The Lord has chosen Israel for His peculiar treasure [29] above all other races that are upon the earth. Israel would be God's servant race [30] in whom God will be glorified. The separations are by geography, as the Most High Creator has made all the tribes/nations of Israel. He has foreordained the appointed national boundaries [31] of where they will be permanently [32]. Restored specifically in America, described as inheriting the desolate heritages [33]. The Lord sent a word unto Jacob, and it hath lighted (fallen) upon Israel [34]. What a blessing to,*"Arise, shine; for thy light is come, and the glory of the Lord is risen upon thee... behold, the darkness* (Baal priests) *shall cover the earth... but the Lord shall arise upon thee, and His glory shall be seen upon thee* (Israel)" [35].

To see, one must look. America is the greatest Christian nation in the history of the world and some Judeo-Christian Baal priest tells you America is not in the Bible. That would be an incredible oversight on God's part would it not? The key of Armageddon dissolves the hogwash of wolves in sheep's clothing, of the pulpit pimps that dream up false doctrines. Who has the Bible in abundance today? Who translates, publishes, distributes and expounds it to the Gentiles (nations)? It is the White race! The Great Commission directed the White disciples in Mark 16:15 to go into all the known world at that time and preach the gospel; but before going to the far reaches, they were to begin with Jerusalem [36] and preach repentance and remission of sins in Jesus name. Then, they were to go to the other nations to be a blessing.

When a White man (Israelite) rejects the good news of his God given identity, he also rejects the blessings from the one and only true God. Do an experiment with Deuteronomy 28. Test each verse as to whether or not these blessings have materialized in America. In Malachi 4:5-6, the spirit or godly motivations of Elijah is turning or teaching the heart or attitude of the fathers (leaders of our nation) to the history of the children of Israel, and the children (Israelites today) towards their fathers (the Old Testament patriarch). If you are seeking the Lord and want to do that which is right, then you will look unto the rock whence you are hewn [37]. By discovering your racial history in the Bible you will find that God called Abraham our father alone and blessed him. If you have not already accepted these truths, look in a mirror and tell yourself you can live without God's gifts.

Chapter 6

Prophecies of Israel

If we are in the latter days of the "end times" as a majority of professing Christians will concur, then prophecy concerning Israel of the Holy Bible (not Talmudic imitators) must coincide with the scriptural descriptions of events that are coming to pass. We can clearly see back into history the slow growth of civilization compared to the phenomenal industrial/technological revolution of America and an acceleration of progress as never before seen. As mentioned earlier in clarifying the differences between the House of Israel and Judah, which is the birthright and scepter, so too are the prophecies distinguishable.

The false claims of Jews being Israel or Judah is not supported by prophecy. However, there are prophecies, identifying those who call themselves Jews today such as: Isaiah 3:9, the Jews to be known by the way they look and behave; this comes about through miscegenation [38], a new racial stock of people returned to Jerusalem after the Babylonian captivity (a minority of the tribe of Benjamin remained racially pure settling in Galilee, keeping the seedline clean for Christ to be born in). It is these mongrel Pharisees that worship the Babylonian Talmud to this day, that Christ so appropriately denounced and could hardly be a part of. The unnatural Jewish nose is a sign that God gives to race mixers. Also Isaiah 65:15, "and ye shall leave your name (Jew) for a curse unto my chosen (Christian). Jeremiah 24:9, the Jews to be scattered in all the kingdoms of the earth for their hurt to be a reproach, a proverb, a taunt and a curse. Jeremiah 15:7, the Jews bereft of children (population statistics do not mark them as the fruitful multitude, stars of heaven).

Jesus *never* called himself a Jew, but He did call the Jews murderers and "of their father, the devil" [39] like sleazy serpents and shady vipers [40]. We must also correct the fallacious notion that our Bible is an offshoot of Judaism. The traditions of the elders made the laws of God ineffective [41] and the oral teachings of these elders were not codified or written until 500 A.D. (known as the Talmud). And today's Torah is a repugnant distortion of the Pentateuch, which is not the Mosaic law Christ came to confirm. The literature of Jews are a compilation of antichrist lies and pusillanimous diatribe. The same divisiveness of today's Judeo-Christian churches tells us that the laws of God are not in effect; therefore the only laws in effect would be man-made. Bible prophecy is inextricably linked to God's servant race Israel obeying and administrating His holy law. Now you can see how critical the identity of His people is.

The Jewish Encyclopedia [42] makes it crystal clear that "Edom is in modern Jewry". Esau is Edom [43]. God loves Jacob and hates Esau [44]; they (Edomite Jews, the mongrel Christ haters) shall build (their modern bandit state in Palestine, thanks to the White American taxpayer), but I (Yahweh) will throw down. Prophecy predicts their destruction. To be allied with the unholy apostate church (Judeo-Christianity) is to bring loss of salvation and eternal damnation. *"My people are destroyed for a lack of knowledge"* [45].

You have been put on notice! It is my prayer that the information contained herein is not a work done in vain. May the Holy Spirit move you to reject the words of the enemy. Much is at stake for the Jewish masterminds to maintain their web of deceit, constantly haranguing the so called "holocaust" of World War II thereby extracting solicitation for materialistic sympathy or else they unleash their rabid mafia front groups to extinguish the spirit of truth. They know that if the truth of 30 million Russian Christians annihilated by communist Jewish butchers were proven (and it has) then their other lies would likewise fall into the gutter where it belongs. Most of the perverted atrocities they falsely accuse others of doing are the product of a demented imagination because of their own propensity for such behavior. They are masters of the smear campaign and character assassination. The wholesale murder and exploitation of White Christians continues unabated. The preceding commentary on Jews was necessary to help the reader identify the counterfeit claims of a Christ hating people that can't possibly fit into the prophecies concerning the real Israel.

America is historically and biblically distinguished as the New Jerusalem, Zion, the wilderness, the desolate heritage, the land of milk and honey, an Israelite kingdom and hence the re-gathering location of Armageddon. Without studious search, there are some Judeo-Christians who can't find the U.S.A. in the Bible. Whether they believe it or not, we are and have been fulfilling Israel's mission and earthly responsibilities.

What happened to the northern house of Israel? They were rooted up and scattered [46] from Samaria to Assyria, and removed them out of His sight [47]. This was the beginning of Israel being lost, with the birthright blessings withheld for a period of time known as "7 times punishment" [48] because they broke the covenant and became divorced with God [49]. What is 7 times? If the disciples would have had the key to understanding prophetic calculation, they wouldn't have asked about the dispersed of Israel being restored in Acts 1:6. The key is found in Revelation 12:6 and 14 where 1,260 days is also called a time, and times and half a time. Figuring a "time" as 360 days or years, according to the day/year punishment calculations of Numbers 14:34 and Ezekiel 4:6, then "times" would be a doubling or 720 and "half a time" 180. Add them up and you get 360+720+180=1,260. This verifies that a "time" is indeed 360 years. So "7 times" is 7 multiplied by 360 which equals 2,520. Israel's deportations into Assyrian captivity was completed in 744 B.C. By subtracting 744 from 2,520 we pass from B.C. dating to A.D. and arrive at the date 1776. Can you think of any nation that was born in that year? In Deuteronomy 32:26 it says people would not remember them (Israelites) because their identity and name were lost (this couldn't apply to Jews as they push their false claims).

47

In II Samuel 7:10, God plants Israel in an appointed place where they will dwell and move no more. That place is referred to as 'the isles' of Isaiah 24:15, 49:1 and Jeremiah 31:10, or better known as the British Isles. It is the land to which Jeremiah brought the throne of David [50], and Zedekiah's daughter to merge with the descendants of Israel described in Genesis 49:22 as 'the fruitful bough'. And these people, our ancestors, would fulfill the prophecy of colonizing the world, becoming a company of nations. It is interesting corroboration that colonial America used the symbol of the eagle with outstretched wings as part of its heraldry found in Exodus 19:4 and Deut. 32:11.

An even more in-depth study will reveal symbols of the tribes of Israel found in the heraldry of White Christian nations today. The woman of Revelation 12:1 and 6 is Israel that fled to the American wilderness, a place prepared of God; v. 14 and given two wings of a great eagle, that it may fly out of its captivity. The birthright blessings were restored after the '7 times punishment' of Israel had expired. In the 1800's, wealth and power blossomed as never before anywhere in the history of mankind! The United States and Great Britain possessed more than 2/3 of all the cultivated resources in the world. Now we are losing it faster than we got it.

This is what happens when we still rebel (repeating history because we haven't learned the truth): God will break the pride of your power [51]. As our flag burns, God will reciprocate our disobedience by making heaven (the sky) as iron and the earth as brass. Rain doesn't fall from iron and a hardened soil doesn't produce crops. How is American agriculture doing? Can you see the prophecy of drought and famine coming to pass? What about our cities? Micah 5:11 predicts decay and destruction because v.12 of the witchcraft (rebellion against God's law) and soothsayers (Hal Lindsey, Van Impe, Billy Graham etc.). This era of world instability that we are going through now, has been identified by some biblical scholars as the 'time of Jacob's trouble' mentioned in Jeremiah 30:7. But we will be saved out of it after we learn our lesson; to be free from the alien races; we must obey the command: ye shall be a separate people [52]. The Old Testament is the New Testament concealed, the New Testament is the Old Testament revealed. And if any man shall take away the words of the book of this prophecy, God will take away his part out of the book of life and out of the holy city, and from the things that are written in this book [53].

Chapter 7

Misnomers and
False Interpretations of Israel

The controversy is between two schools of eschatology (study of the end times); that of the historicists and futurists. The former, as the name implies, explains God's Word in sacred and secular history, both of which is His Story. The Protestant reformers understood correctly, events that had come to pass fulfilling the veracity of scriptures. On the other hand, the futurist disregard the past and place the works of God in the distant future.

Futurism is the greatest mental block which people have against accepting our identity as Israel. These wolves in sheep's clothing defend their errors as if they were defending their inheritance. But in fact, they are denying their actual biblical birthright. Their doctrines were devised by papal Rome to regain control over people through fear that they enjoyed during the Dark Ages. The futurist use clever buzzwords like: the rapture, the battle of Armageddon, the coming antichrist, pre, mid and post tribulation, Israeli, Zionist,

Judeo-Christian ethic, Christian Jews, Gentiles, the holocaust, anti-semitic... ad nauseam.

The Lord pictured two types of people in this era: the ones with their hearts failing them for fear – looking after that which is coming [54] and the others who joyfully stand uplifted anticipating deliverance (v. 28). The pulpit pimps and TV preachers would tell "us" that the tribulation will be the most diabolical time ever, when "they" shall escape it, as God removes them from earth. This is a lie and diversion from the millions of Christian martyrs murdered since the time of Christ [55], but it is to our glory that God works in the lives of His true people [56], whereby the truth is perfectly interpreting and rightly dividing His Word that will set us free as we see the keys to the puzzle fit together, slowly bringing the big picture into focus. The apostle John wrote of 'great tribulation' [57], which has lasted throughout the whole of the Christian dispensation. It is folly to try to crowd into 1/2 or even 7 years, a time of trouble as mentioned in the book of Revelation. It would tax the ingenuity of man to imagine all that Christians have gone through for their faith. Paul also taught we must go through much tribulation to enter the Kingdom [58]. Myriads of blood-washed souls have passed through these fires of suffering that futurists would rather keep quiet. If we were living in certain parts of the world, ruled by hardened hearts (modern pharaohs), we as Christians would have no doubts about when things begin to tribulate. A change of residence would change the theology and status of many deluded believers with their sights yet in the future. The liars have much to lose and will not recant. Thirty million Christians have died in this century alone at the bloody hands of red Edomite Jew communists since the Talmudic/Bolshevik Revolution of 1917. If the meaning of words and identity of who's who in the Bible are twisted to such an extent, then the people are bound to a propaganda tantamount to brainwashing.

The Bible speaks of *many* being deceived [59], even those in positions of authority. Just because the majority of churches believe that today's Jews are the biblical Israelites, does not make it so. At one time it was dangerous to deny the earth was flat, however truth is not determined by popular consensus. There is ample documentation from Jewish authorities themselves that say they are not a Semitic people (descendant of Shem); but assume this identity for political and economic expediency. Some say that Jews are not a race, but rather a mere religion. Why then do they attach their name, when supposedly converting to Christianity? We don't have Islamic or Hindu Christians, nor can there be Christian Jews any more than there can be cold fire or dry water. What better way for the enemies of Christ to exploit His followers, than to be accepted by manipulating the names Jew with Christian [60].

The false prophets' agenda conforms to political ambitions, a new age and world order with false Christs, ignoring biblical timing, people and geography; and hysterically demanding the defense of the Zionist state (on stolen Palestinian property) at all costs, saying that Russia will invade Israelie (their battle of Armageddon hoax). If Christians would but understand the differences between the Seventy Weeks of Daniel 9:24-27, the Tribulation of John's revelation and the Time of Jacob's Trouble described in Jeremiah 30:4-10 rather than taking the arbitrary word of futurists, much about God's Word would be clarified (when you read, study and pray for the Holy Spirit to lead you to truth). But where are the Soviet missiles aimed at today? Communism is not dead as long as Judaism exists!

That Great Day of the Lord will separate the wheat from the tares, and the non-Christian tares (those impersonating wheat or the true Israel) will be removed from off the face of the earth (raptured!) by casting them into the fiery furnace [61]. Christianity stands in the way of the internationalist plans for the would-be gods. It is the Aryan Israelite race that God predestined for Western Christian civilization to be a blessing to the nations [62] and salt of the earth [63], preserving His laws, statutes and commandments. The enemies of God want to eliminate God's law of segregation so that the despoilers miscegenate all races and homogenize all religions into one mongrelized United Nations. The U.N. is just another tower of Babel (confusion).

To those who say, "suppose we are Israel, what difference does it make"? I say it makes all the difference in the world (kosmos – the social order). If you don't care, you're no different than the reprobate Esau or the traitorous Judas. You open the floodgates for evil to prosper when you nonchalantly reject the truth, and the truth sets us free. Will you throw this God given gift away or will you be one of the few that enters the narrow gate and finds the way to life? The purveyors of disinformation are the opposite of I Thessalonians

5:21. They don't prove anything because there is no goodness in them. Woe unto the sophists of futurism. Beware of misnomers.

Chapter 8

Migrations of Israel

In Matthew 13:44, the Kingdom of heaven is like unto treasure. Israel is the Lord's peculiar treasure[64] hidden in a field. The field is the world[65]. Jesus is the buyer of the lost tribes of Israel hidden in the world at the cost of His precious blood [66]. This treasure He found and then hid in the field before He purchased the field (world). Why was Israel lost in the world? Could it be so that they could be properly identified and delivered?

Many good intentions of the churches, for which the road to hell is paved, mistakenly think that Jesus came to save everybody on earth. A favorite scripture for the integrationists to rationalize that all races are one in Christ is Galatians 3:28-29 when they magically defy the laws of inheritance and genetics. The problem words are 'Jew' and 'Greek', which are simply the tribe of Judah and tribes of Israel in Greece respectively. If Paul had meant other races, to make his point, why didn't he say Ethiopian or Canaanite? Verse two does not say, 'Wherefore the law was everybody's schoolmaster to bring everybody unto Christ, that everybody might be justified by faith'. The context is *racial* Israel.

All 12 tribes of Israel are one in Christ. Jesus says in Matthew 15:24, that He was sent only unto the lost sheep of the house of Israel. Israelites in scripture have always been one race of people and referred to as His sheep. John 10:27 says that His sheep hear His voice. What race of people have historically been the followers of Christ and responsible for the advancement of Christianity? The Anglo Saxon and kindred folk of course! But Israel became scattered from the Assyrian captivity [67], not to be confused with the Babylonian captivity. Luke 1:68 declares the God of Israel redeeming His people to keep His racial promises and covenants (verses 72-73), and improves upon it with the New Covenant [68], again exclusively with the houses of Israel and Judah (not Jews). Israel did not return to Samaria. Judah did return a remnant to Jerusalem.

So where did the Israelites go after the Assyrian empire fell? Some seminary-fed ministers parrot the line that they disappeared or intermarried with other races. This babble reflects their ability to make God a liar and for scriptures to disappear. As to the Israelites whereabouts, the Lord says in Amos 9:9 that He would sift the house of Israel among the nations, like corn sifted in a sieve, and not one seed shall fall to the ground. Their racial stock shall remain intact. After all, God promised their fathers Abraham, Isaac and Jacob the blessing of being a great multitude; a population numbered as the stars of heaven; the sand upon the sea shore and as the dust of the earth.

The historian Josephus reaffirms the existence of the 10 tribes and their inestimable numbers at the time of Christ [69]. During the Assyrian captivity, God no longer pleaded with Israel. He divorced Israel because of their disobedience and whoring after other gods. They no longer qualified or deserved His blessing. He left them a slave people, left to their own devices. They even lost their Hebrew language. They erroneously regarded themselves as gentiles and so did the world. But Jesus Christ knew where the lost were [70], and commanded the 12 disciples to go to them (Israel), not to the gentiles (heathen) or Samaritans (non-Israelites). Why are the 12 tribes greeted in James 1:1? Israel was scattered abroad physically (and may have been scatterbrained spiritually as well) as sheep without a shepherd [71]. The Israelites would eventually dwell in a predestined location [72] after their fall, captivity and dispersion.

They were the dispersed (Israelites) among the gentiles (Greeks) referred to in John 7:35.

It would help you to look at some good biblical maps to get an idea of how millions of our race were deported from ancient Israel to Assyria (modern Syria and Turkey) and from there (after the fall of the Assyrian empire) were left no other choice but to migrate north and west, uniquely and carefully being led by providence. The Lord locates, filters and leads them [73] along the countries of the northern Mediterranean and into all of Europe.

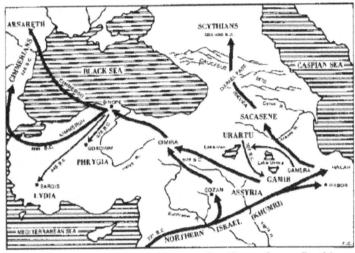

Israel – Gamera – Gimera – Kimmeroii – Cimmerians – Scythians

The above map shows the early migrations of the Israelites from Ancient Israel to Assyria. The map below shows the migrations after the downfall of the Assyrian Empire. The Israelites went north and west to settle what we now call Europe.

ISRAEL'S WANDERINGS.

The intricate name changes and fascinating archaeology of cuneiform clay tablets impart an accurate history of the true Israel lost and found. If we trace back through White European cultures [74] and go forward in time identifying the Israelitish cultures [75] from the Assyrian records, then the so-called missing links are resolved. The emerging settlements of Europe were in fact the colonization of migrating tribes of Israel; becoming many nations [76]. Israelites in Europe were not only being preserved by God but were also establishing permanent residences [77]. It was all part of God's plan, that only God could orchestrate [78]. The Good Shepherd gathering and bringing His sheepfold to their own land.

Where was the first Christian church? The early Christians in Palestine were underground because of persecution and Roman Catholicism was not founded until about 350 A.D. (although Paul dedicated the home of Pudens and Claudia as a place to worship in Rome in 56 A.D.). Thanks to Joseph of Arimathea, Britain was the first of all kingdoms to receive the Gospel. This was confirmed by the Church Councils of Pisa (1409), Constance (1417), Sienna (1424) and Basle (1434) that maintained, "the churches of France and Spain, must yield in point of antiquity and precedence to that of Britain, as the latter church was founded by Joseph of Arimathea immediately after the passion of Christ".

Many church historians date the good news of the Gospels reaching Britain around the time of the death of Tiberius Caesar in 37 A.D. and flourished thereafter with the building of the first Christian church erected above ground in 39-41 A.D. at Glastonbury. This is not worthy of debate; it is indisputable historical fact. Britan or the 'isles of the sea' [79] has the most endearing Christian history from which we can glean understanding of what the Bible is all about. The British royal family documents its lineage to King David [80]. It was Jeremiah that brought the daughters of Zedikiah to Ireland [81] and Jacob's pillar stone which is placed in the Coronation Chair to this day [82].

In 1320 A.D. Robert Bruce proclaimed the Scottish Declaration of Independence wherein, "the nation of Scots... which passing from the greater Scythia (the Assyrian territories where Israel was placed in about 700 B.C.)... by many victories and infinite toil, acquired for themselves the possessions in the West". There is an abundance of legend kept alive for millennia, yet suppressed by black-robed apostates, that Mary, the mother of Jesus, died in Britain and is buried at Glastonbury, and that Paul and other apostles and disciples preached in Britain and Europe. To complete the migrations of Israel, it is now becoming obvious that the U.S.A. is most definitely a key participant. Read, if you will, the Mayflower Compact of 1620: "Having undertaken for the glory of God and the advancement of the Christian faith"; and the Constitution of the New England Confederation of 1643: "Whereas we all came into these parts of America with one and the same end and aim, namely to advance the Kingdom of our Lord Jesus Christ."

The sure Word of God specifies where that Kingdom will be in the prophecy of Israel's re-gathering (remember the true meaning of Armageddon); in Micah 4:8 that Kingdom will come to the daughter of Jerusalem and not the old mother. A second witness is Jesus telling the filthy Jews in Matthew 21:43 that their kingdom would be taken away from them and given to a nation bringing forth the fruits thereof. The daughter of Zion or the new political enforcement of God's laws is the pretext for the theocracy of Christ headquartered in America – not Tel Aviv where you will never hear the Christ-hating Jews proclaiming "No King but Jesus!" The Kingdom of Heaven is like a treasure hid in a field. You won't find it, if you don't look.

Chapter 9

Judgments of Israel

Proof that we are still God's covenant people is that we are still chastised. For whom the Lord loveth He chasteneth [83]. Our endurance and developing discipline from the chastening receives us to Almighty God as His sons [84] in order to break the spirit of rebellion, to bring repentance [85], and to return to the teachings of obeying the Law [86]. America is being chastised because we are Israel and the sons of God. Bastards or non-Israelites are not chastised [87]. In America, our beginning was blessed (annuit coeptis) as we discerned in chapter 3, but now we are cursed for not opposing the satanic Jew. Wrath is upon us if we help or love those who hate the Lord [88]. 'Hate the sin, but love the sinner' is a nonsensical cliché that is not found in the Bible.

We have not heeded the wisdom of Benjamin Franklin who allegedly said in 1787 at the Philadelphia Constitutional Convention,

"I fully agree with George Washington, that we must protect this young nation from an insidious influence and impenetration. That menace, gentlemen, is the Jews. If you do not exclude them from these United States, in this Constitution, in less than 200 years they will dominate and devour the land and change our form of government... In whatever country Jews have settled in any great number, they have lowered its moral tone, depreciated its commercial integrity... and have sneered at and tried to undermine the Christian religion upon which that nation is founded."

When the alien parasite has consumed the host (when welfare and foreign aid is sucked dry) the vampire will turn to other victims, seeing the great curse of Israel's God [89]. Because Christians have forsaken the racial covenants of the Lord of their fathers, we see the judgments upon us. The defamation of attaching Judeo before Christian is a self inflicted oxymoron. The alien brings philosophies of 'higher criticism' (pseudo intellectuals) and pagan heresies to Christian doctrine. We have strayed from our Christian forefather's way of life when the laws of God were administered as the law of the land. We are not to degenerate into democracy, whereby mob rule dictates golden calves. Just because a majority decides upon a moral issue does not make it right. God made this point with Sodom and Gomorah.

There is only one righteousness and that is found in the deity of Jesus Christ [90]. Ezekiel prophesied the future judgment of Israel in 20:33-38 where God gathers Israel out of slavery again (the persecution of Protestants in Europe)... "with fury poured out" refers to the vials of wrath in Revelation 16 (of which we find the all important word Armageddon in verse 16)... and there in the wilderness [91] of America, God will plead with the regathered tribes of Israel.

This is why we need to know our identity, to respond to His rod and know that He is our father in heaven. The purpose and result of punishment is correction, to lift us up from the cesspool of subhuman decadence to which our race, nation and faith has sunk. Correction means repentance or making changes, to go the other way, the right way. To not do the things we think are right [92], but to do what God's Word says is right.

When we fail to execute a killer or rapist because we believe in the goodness of man, we reap what we sow if we parole that killer and he repeats the crime again. If His people reject the idea of an inherent sinful nature, then they would also reject the idea of Christ's blood sacrifice for the remission of their sins, for their transgression of the Law [93]. For them, the crucifixion was in vain. It is my earnest prayer that those of us who take the scriptures seriously, should now bow down on our knees and take to heart and mind and soul II Chronicles 7:14.

Chapter 10

Regathering of the Lost Tribes

The absolute miracle of God's dynamic drive to lead His people to be gathered is a logistical wonder to behold that only an omniscient, omnipotent and omnipresent God could perform. His story (history) has not been left to chance or accident. Zechariah 10:10 says the Lord gathered them out of Assyria; in verse 7-8, Ephraim (a son of Joseph, whose identity marks, blessings and prophecies point to Britain) is gathered, redeemed and increased.

We will be spared and restored. God "will gather you from the people, and assemble you out of the countries where ye have been scattered (the old world, Europe), and I will give you the land of Israel (the new world, America)", where we will be a judged and converted remnant [94]. In Nehemiah 1:8-9, the principle found is that if you disobey, He scatters and if you obey, He gathers.

In the I Chronicle 16:35 psalm of David, 'being saved' is being gathered together and delivered from the heathen; not floating up to heaven with the heathens. The covenant to gather Israel is in

Deuteronomy 30:1-3, and it shall come to pass. God calls His people to help them, *"Gather my saints together... those that have made a covenant with me"* [95]. Even though there has been chastisement, it is with great mercies that He, as a husband, gathers us [96]. As the Lord gathers His remnant back to the fold, they shall be fruitful and multiply, and have shepherds (ministers) to protect them in their own land [97]. The beautiful words of Joel 2:15-16 tells us of the people being gathered for a solemn assembly... for a marriage; and in verse 17, a prayer to spare our inheritance from reproach (shameful disgrace by rejecting our God-given heritage) when the heathen rules over us and asks 'where is your God'? where we can unashamedly say, as found in v.27, that He is in the midst of Israel.

There are numerous gatherings that span the centuries and will culminate in Armageddon, i.e. America, as the location for the tribes of Israel to be gathered together. God has a plan and purpose in relation to the grand scale mobilizations of so many people. The ratio of White Americans to non-Whites in this country is rapidly changing and along with it, the moral complexion. Conditions are reaching a crescendo of confrontation as predicted in Joel 3:2 and 9. Several factions are maneuvering and preparing for a racial war. As stated in v. 16-17, our strength and hope is through God and the holiness of His law and order, which prohibits so-called peaceful coexistence with strange gods of the aliens corrupting our nation. Our Christian duty is to declare war on the wickedness that prevails unabated [98]. Let it be known, we are to warn unbelievers and those who stand in the way of righteousness, that they shall surely die as a consequence of their lawlessness [99]. God has chosen this land and people to fulfill: to chase the moneychangers out of our national institutions. We are supposed to wake up to the abominations (mixing the holy with the profane) here and now [100].

We need to examine our relationship with Jesus Christ, if we are to be living and reigning with Him [101]. The confirmation of Christ's sacrifice, not just for Israel alone, but in order to gather the scattered into one [102] has happened in America. This marvelous gathering is all in preparation for the return of Christ in which the Lord separates His sheep from the goats and blesses His true Chosen with their Kingdom inheritance [103]. Praise the King of Kings power to gather... all glory be unto the Lord of Lords.

Chapter 11

The Kingdom

Seek ye first the Kingdom [104] and after that, God will provide what you need. When mankind realizes that his priorities are not in harmony with God's priorities, then we shall become God fearing men and women and begin to understand (Proverbs 9:10) that love is obeying the commandments of God [105]. Are you pleasing God or yourself with your thoughts and actions?

A Kingdom has four components: land, people, laws and a King. The Kingdom of God is thus: 1. The land belongs to God forever [106]; 2. God has chosen Israel to be His people above all other races in the earth [107]; 3. God's laws have dominion over a man as long as he lives [108]; and 4. Jesus is proclaimed King [109].

Armageddon is good, and will lead us to a new age and a new world order with Jesus Christ claiming His throne in glory where every knee shall bow. It will mean the end of the traditions of today's pharisees and Talmudic life. The regathering will restore the preserved of Israel, the salt of the earth, thy judges and counselors.

We will be administrating Romans 13, not legislating the traditions of man or Jewish fables. The wise and understanding men of Israel (not the political race mixers) will be the captains and officers ruling over the tribes [110]. A wonderful remarriage is predestined between the God of Israel and the Bride of Christ (Israel / White Christians) [111].

We Anglo Saxon, Scandinavian, Germanic and kindred people were separated for the purpose of forming the original nucleus for the Kingdom of God on earth, under the kingship of the Lord Jesus Christ. And the den of vipers (jews) who have consistently and continually rejected our Savior are shallow and pathetic impersonators. The White Christian nations were to be the model state to give a practical example to the rest of the world. Not until they become what God ordained for them, will the rest of the world want God's way [112].

Obviously, God made a specific difference between the Israel people and the rest of the world. No amount of U.N. interference, Congressionally passed anti-hate crime laws or court decisions can change the Divine decree. God has decreed we shall be the head and not the tail. The sooner we recognize our role and act upon it, the better it will be for us and others. The rulers of darkness probably know and understand the biblical formula for the Kingdom of God better than the true Israel that it was intended for. This explains their barrage of circumventing the scriptures at every turn and deceiving all nations with their sorceries [113] and of all that were slain by the great men of the earth. We know who these prostitutes are in government, churches, banks, schools and commerce [114]. We know them by their fruits (what they produce), drunken on the blood of the saints, waxed rich from abominations and blasphemy, the hypocrites that devour widow's house [115].

The lamenting prayer of Jeremiah cries, "Thou, O Lord, remainest for ever; thy throne from generation to generation. Wherefore dost thou forget us for ever, and forsake us so long a time. Turn thou us unto thee, O Lord, and we shall be turned; renew our days as of old" [116]. For years, patriotic Christians have been endeavoring to solve our mounting problems without getting at the causes. Only a cursory diagnosis is applied to the symptoms. How much more suffering must we endure, because of our blindness to who we are and our responsibility to God? We have a destiny that we cannot avoid or evade. We are God's servant race Israel; in the building of a Kingdom of righteousness here on earth.

Our identity is the vision of the standard-bearer radiating the light of Christ, fearlessly crusading the message of the good news of the gospel. We are the same heirs today, that Paul witnessed to his brethren; his kinsmen by race, who are Israelites: to whom rightfully belongs the adoption, the glory, the covenants, the law giving, the service of God and the promises; of whom were the fathers, of whose race the Messiah became incarnate above all [117]. Let us rejoice in Armageddon and seek His Kingdom, believing in His good, noble and perfect will for us.

"And God shall wipe away all the tears from their eyes... neither shall there be any more pain" [118].

Endnotes and Scripture References:

1. Strong's Concordance #717
2. Strong's Concordance #2022
3. Strong's Concordance #4023
4. From *gadad*, Strong's Concordance #1413 - to crowd, assemble or gather together
5. Psalm 147:19-20
6. Isaiah 2:12 and II Peter 3:10
7. I Corinthians 6:9-10 and Revelation 21:8
8. Matthew 13:11
9. Proverbs 25:2
10. Romans 12:2
11. Joshua 24:15
12. Revelation 18:20
13. Revelation 18:11, 18
14. Jeremiah 23:22
15. Isaiah 42:19 and 43:10
16. Romans 11:25
17. Ezra 2:64
18. John 10:26-27
19. Exodus 31:13
20. Luke 1:32- 33

21. John 3:13
22. Matthew 24:31
23. Name another nation, other than Great Britain, that has great in its name.
24. Romans 9:2
25. Psalm 147:19-20
26. Hebrews 8:10
27. Numbers 23:9
28. Leviticus 20:24 and I Kings 8:53
29. Psalm 135:4 and Deut. 14:2
30. Isaiah 45:4 and 49:3
31. Acts 17:26
32. II Samuel 7:10 and I Chronicles 17:19
33. Isaiah 49:8 and 35:1
34. Isaiah 9:8
35. Isaiah 60:1-2
36. Luke 24:47
37. Isaiah 51:1-2
38. Nehemiah 13:23
39. John 8:44
40. Matthew 23:33
41. Matthew 15:2, 6
42. Jewish Encyclopedia, vol. 5, p. 41, 1925
43. Genesis 36:1
44. Malachi 1:3-4
45. Hosea 4:6
46. I Kings 14:15
47. II Kings 17:18
48. Leviticus 26:18, 21, 24, 28
49. Jeremiah 3:8
50. The scepter or Jacob's pillar stone is located within the royal coronation chair to this day.
51. Leviticus 26:19
52. Exodus 33:16
53. Revelation 22:19
54. Luke 21:26
55. John 16:33
56. Romans 5:3
57. Revelation 6:9-10, 7:14
58. Acts 14:22
59. Matthew 24:5, 11, 24
60. Matthew 24:5

61. Matthew 13:42
62. Genesis 12:2-3
63. Matthew 5:13
64. Psalm 135:4
65. Matthew 13:38
66. I Peter 1:19
67. Jeremiah 50:17
68. Hebrews 8:8,10
69. Antiquities of the Jews, Book XI, chapter V
70. Matthew 10:5-6
71. Matthew 9:36
72. II Samuel 7:10
73. Ezekiel 36:19,24
74. Saxons,Vikings, Gauls, Celts, Cimbri, Goths, Teutons, etc.
75. Scythians, Cimmerians, Saka, Gimir, Khumri, etc.
76. Genesis 17:4
77. Isaiah 49:8
78. Ezekiel 34:13
79. Isaiah 24:15, 49:1
80. Psalm 89:35-37
81. This is Ezekiel's riddle of chapter 17
82. Genesis 35:11
83. Hebrews 12:6
84. Proverbs 3:11-12
85. Revelation 3:19
86. Psalm 94:12
87. Hebrews 12:8
88. II Chronicles 19:2
89. Deuteronomy 29:22-25
90. John 1:1-14
91. Ezekiel 20:35
92. Proverbs 14:12
93. I John 3:4, Hebrews 9:22
94. Ezekiel 11:17, 20:34, 41
95. Psalm 50:5
96. Isaiah 54:5, 7
97. Jeremiah 23:3-4, 8
98. Psalm 149:5-9; Matthew 10:34
99. Ezekiel 3:18-19
100.Isaiah 52:1-3
101. Revelation 20:4
102.John 11:50-52

103. Matthew 25:31-34
104. Matthew 6:33
105. I John 5:3
106. Leviticus 25:23
107. Leviticus 26:12, Deut. 7:6, II Cor. 6:16
108. Romans 7:1
109. John 12:13, 15
110. Deut. 1:13-15
111. Revelation 21:9, 12
112. Isaiah 2:1-5
113. Revelation 18:23-24
114. Matthew 7:16-20
115. Luke 20:47
116. Lamentations 5:19-21
117. Romans 9:3-5
118. Revelation 21:4

Chapter 12

In Defense of Legends

Are legends Christian? Some people don't think so. A legend is a story coming down from the past, especially one popularly regarded as historical although not verifiable. 'Prima scriptura', which holds that the Bible is the primary source of doctrine, but that understanding can be improved by reference to other sources. 'Sola scriptura', on the other hand, a product of the Protestant Reformation, leaves us a legacy that has evolved from the original protest against church authority, in contradistinction to the Bible itself having sole authority. A legend can be either good or bad, true or false. The point to remember is that it is something that is passed down generationally. Of course, God's Word is the final authority; it's just what you do with it.

Should each of us be able to read the Bible for ourselves, now that we have printing presses, and comparatively evaluate the merits of both the church and the reformers? The motivations of Catholicism and Eastern Orthodoxy have epitomized their theology with the embodiment of a deity or spirit in some earthly form to translate not only the Bible, but also the prayers and liturgies, among other things, of the church. This extra-biblical shove in a particular direction is the stuff in which legends are born by the manipulative machinations of those who would reject other legends outside the textual criticism of the Bible and exist through time till it is either proven or dispelled. A lot of legends die an ignoble death, while others persist for centuries. One could say that it is a war of legends, a war between good and evil. The principle of a legend will survive because people are attracted to its premise. A good example of this fratricidal conflict is in Northern Ireland.

As John Wesley stated in the 18th century, "The Church is to be judged by the Scriptures, not the Scriptures by the Church." The premise is that the Scriptures are guaranteed to remain true to their divine source, and thus, only insofar as the Church retains scriptural faith is it assured of all the promises of God. Likewise, if Catholic/Orthodoxy were to become the biblically predicted apostate church, which many have affirmed, then its authority would be null and void. Their own legends become their own worst enemy. What follows is a legendary church claiming itself as the source of truth, much to the chagrin of a sordid history. As a consequence, profound doubts emerge after a millennial of abuse and begins another millennia of damage control. It goes way beyond the intent of the Protestant Reformation and I believe is the hand of God at work. The more the state sanctioned institutions called "churches" fall away from God's authority and relegate it to themselves, can we witness their piety of whited sepulchers and a holier-than-thou corpus. Ye shall know them by their fruits and their fruit is rigor mortis.

Is the body of Bible believing Christians capable of taking care of itself, or are we so spiritually challenged that we need a class of priests to tell us what to think? I thought the Levitical was replaced with the Melchisedec, where every man is a priest unto God, but apparently, the Levitical legend lives on in the priest-craft of assumed orthodoxy.

This priesthood of self-proclaimed *authority* can then create or destroy whatever legend they deem fit for serving their special interests. If so much legend of authority is attributed to the almighty church and its army of priests, then why is there a need for the Holy Spirit? I'll tell you why. Our race has been in bondage to the apostate church for so long, that it is stymied in its growth and maturing in Christ. Rather than chewing strong spiritual meat, the orthodoxies have fed milk, or in some cases, spiritual cyanide to a baby believer. They are not allowed to think or live as God intended; to be aware of Christian legends that would free them from the yoke of a medicating clergy. "For by thy sorceries were all nations deceived."

The truth of what is considered the church is nothing more than a fictional legend, a contraption of corporate Babylon and has no semblance to the biblical *ecclesia* or the first century apostolics. Legends of the early body of Christ was a body politic more concerned with the advancement of the Kingdom of God, than with the advancement of man made institutions under the guise of religion.

How has the elite class of "Father-priests" made any difference, "That we henceforth be no more children, tossed to and fro, and carried about with every wind of doctrine, by the sleight of men, and cunning craftiness"? Where is their fruit? Where is the fulfillment of "Till we all come in the unity of the faith" when the elitists manipulate the flow of information/understanding and prevent unity? For 500 years, since the Protestant movement began, the Catholic/Orthodox "church" is probably worse off now than then, because of the ruling priesthoods. Priestly censors have robbed the White race of its Christian legends.

How did God intend for His people to respond to their divine calling? To submit to a universalist theology for all races and nations? No. If we compare Eph. 4:12 with 4:16, they are one and the same describing, *"For the perfecting of the saints, for the work of the ministry, for the edifying of the body of Christ"* and, *"From whom the whole body fitly joined together and compacted by that which every joint supplieth, according to the effectual working in the measure of every part, maketh increase of the body unto the edifying of itself in love."* Spiritual growth occurs through our relationship with other Christians, not time spent in cathedrals listening to the vain repetitions of costumed and staged liturgies. When Christian unity grows in the body of Christ, the priesthood is indubitably absent.

White Christians are all called to proclaim the Good News of the gospels. The good news is the *identity* for which this message is intended. The purpose of any ministry is to call back into union and friendship the affections of man towards God, which have been alienated and mongrelized. Anything above or beyond this is a ministry that has no purpose except self-aggrandizement.

The legends that could rekindle a love of God and racial brethren are the ministering of many Christian Identity believers. We believe the legends, because the legends are good. They harmonize with Scripture, not as canon, but as, in many cases, prophetic fulfillment. What good is a prophecy from God, if God's people cannot see its manifestation? *"It is the glory of God to conceal a thing, but the honor of kings is to search out a matter"* –Prov. 25:2. Notice, that it does not say God conceals His Word, but rather a "thing", which could suggest a historical event that is preserved in legend.

God never intended for His plan and purposes to end with keeping His Word, the Bible, in isolation, confined within the four walls of a church building. *"For the Kingdom of God is not in word, but in power"* –I Cor. 4:19. We are also well aware of the fact that, *"The Kingdom of Heaven suffereth violence, and the violent take it by force"* –Mt. 11:12. Hence, the bloody history of the false church.

But the Word and our legends from the past will overcome the lies and treachery. Evidence that God can and does conceal things, only to have them revealed at His appointed times, proves that there are other sources in God's arsenal of eternal wisdom than the 'prima scriptura'. *"And it shall come to pass in the last days, saith God, I will pour out My Spirit upon all flesh and your sons and your daughters shall prophesy, and your young men shall see visions and your old men shall dream dreams"* –Acts 2:17. Knowledge of events of times past, considered legend, can then take their rightful seat of understanding and righteousness, without the hindrance of false prophets and churches.

Who would blind our race to these historical realities? It would be the legion of hysterical adversaries to Christian Identity. They come in all stripes and colors, but they all share a common animus. This is what the satanic realm of humanity is composed of. The tool of their authority is the rewriting of history and the reinvention of Christianity to suit their quest for power. The legends, which

Christian Identity holds dear, will be our connection to the past that shall make our people free. We know that White history is in the rapacious clutches of the antichrist historians of academia and the seminary lapdogs are not far behind. Is it any wonder then that false legends have been created to overshadow true legends?

Even after 1000 years of superficial transformation, the infrastructure of the institutionalized church remains static. It is in the business of promoting men who have a propensity to control other people in behalf of the church. It is also in the business of racial amalgamation as the myth and legend of *universalism*. Therefore, satan/the adversaries of God, are conceptually alive and well in the Catholic/Orthodox people themselves.

Consider the grassroots foundation of Christian Identity, much like the original church, compared to the foundations of other traditions that use and exploit the name Christian. Power from the latter comes from the ecclesiastical hierarchy and trickles down to the parish. Whereas, Christian Identity is moving towards the home church, home schooling, home birthing and getting off the religious grid. It is a paradigm shift from church corporations to kindred clans. It is a discovery of the legends of Glastonbury, the daughter of Zedekiah and Jeremiah in early Irish history, the Coronation Stone, the Wattle church of Jesus in England, Joseph of Arimathea, the travels of Paul, Mary, and others to Europe and the Isles and many more too numerous to expound upon in this article. The point is, these legends are suppressed for a reason; and the reason is that the devilish churches have a lot to lose if White people come to understand that the establishment churches have been a fraud for 1800 years; and a dismal failure at bringing forth the fruits of the Kingdom of God. They will not forfeit their hold on power and thus will remain contrary to the will of God.

God raises up movements to hold up a mirror to the false churches and to preserve the legends of Christianity, which fly in the face of universalism. Churchianity has little resemblance to the church of the Bible or legend. Unless radical changes move the spirit of men, the purpose of the church will remain in the hands of man and not God. It is too great a loss for them to give their entire lives over to God. *"Know ye not, that to whom ye yield yourselves servants to obey, his servants ye are to whom ye obey, whether of sin unto death, or of obedience unto righteousness?"* –Rom. 6:16. What's missing is Christians who will lead by example, rather than by control. Give the legends a chance and don't be persuaded by overbearing elitists. Our legends are rich in substance and principle. They prove our identity as the true Israel of Scripture. The alternative legends of the Roman and Eastern Church prove only a malevolent grab for what belongs to God. The judeo-Christian churches are just cookie-cutter religions of the aforementioned and not much better.

Christian Identity offers our race a plan the way God intended. Our only choice is to come out of Mystery Babylon, the cheap imitations lacking in substance and resolve for century upon century. It will take men and women of courage, rather than playing it safe with government approved religions, to overcome the adversaries of our race. But rest assured, Babylon will fall, *"Because she made all nations drink the wine of the wrath of her fornication"* –Rev. 14:8. The false church has been sabotaging and subverting the White race for far too long; and it is time for the pendulum to swing.

Chapter 13

The Meaning of Kinsman Redeemer

After contemplating what to call our church and website, we kept coming back to the recurrent theme of Kinsman Redeemer. The magnetic appeal of this special concept of Christianity is found in the nature of its exclusivity. It only pertains to the people of the Book; the Israel race comprised of the Anglo Saxon, Celtic, Scandinavian, Germanic and kindred folk. It does not apply to the jews or the other races.

The words *kinsman* and *redeemer* dovetail and are in fact inseparable when discussing this biblical doctrine. They must go together or the integrity of this subject crumbles and the message to God's people is lost. We are the lost sheep of the House of Israel because there are so many shepherds whose only skill is to fleece the flock. *"For the Son of man is come to seek and to save that which was lost"* –Luke 19:10.

The shame of these universalists, and even the race traitors within Identity who teach that salvation and redemption is designed for all the races of the earth, is that they knowingly and willingly spiritualize the recipients of God's design. They include those for whom God never intended to receive the things which are holy. *"Give not that which is holy unto the dogs"* –Mt. 7:6.

Modernized Christianity is a distortion of the Divine Plan for the Ages. It's called the theology of dispensationalism, which means, according to the pulpit pimps, dispense or distribute the Word of God to different people (other than Israel) throughout different periods of history. The method of their madness is to suggest that God changed His mind about the covenants and promises so that non-Israelites could now share in the blessings and gifts. This sort of racial amalgamation is in harmony with jewish communism and the redistribution of not only wealth, but moral values and ethics as well. However, the God of Jacob/Israel says, *"I change not, therefore ye sons of Jacob are not consumed"* –Malachi 3:6. Evil men who try to change and pervert our understanding of God also want to homogenize societies throughout the world so that they can play god and control all peoples.

The deception is in spiritualizing who Israel is; and the meaning of "redeemed." The truth is, God has always discriminated between the races. The Big Lie is, "God loves everybody." It would behoove students of the Bible to find out who God *hates* – whom He hath indignation forever. Most of churchianity does not know what 'kinsman redeemer' means. Their limited understanding may advocate the fiction of an equality of the races, but is far from the realities of biblical predestination and the history of mankind. God has a very special plan. Those who know and love what kinsman redeemer really means, also knows what God's plan and purpose is.

Let us now proceed to define our terms in a scholarly manner. Let us pray for the sheeple that have wandered from the judaized denominations, that this message will strike a chord in their Aryan hearts and the scales will fall from their eyes, and that they will come out of the apostasy that plagues our race. Lord we pray that these brethren come to realize that their so-called relationship with Christ has been superficial and rebellious; and that now, the door of truth has been unlocked and opened to make them free from the world. Amen.

KINSMAN. From Websters 1847 dictionary, *kinsman* is simply defined as "a man of the same race or family; one related by blood." From *Strong's Concordance*, the Hebrew word for *kinsman* is ga'al (#1350) and means "to redeem, i.e. to be the next of kin (and as such to buy back a relative's property, marry his widow, etc.): avenger, deliver, purchase, ransom, revenger." In another source, "it referred originally to the duty of every tribesman, or clansman, to support or avenge the cause of his tribe, clan or family."

REDEEMER. Again, from Websters 1847, *redeemer* is "one who redeems; the Savior of the world, Jesus Christ." Re-deemed means, "to purchase back; to liberate or rescue from captivity or bondage; to rescue and deliver from the bondage of sin and the penalties of God's violated law by obedience and suffering in the place of the sinner, or by doing and suffering that which is accepted in lieu of the sinner's obedience."

"Christ has redeemed us from the curse of the law, being made a curse for us" – Galatians 3:13.

With particular interest, we discover from *Strong's Concordance* that the Hebrew word for *redeemer* is ga'al (#1350). Sound familiar? In fact, the words kinsman and redeemer are the same Hebrew word – ga'al. *Redeemer* means to act the part of a kinsman and *kinsman* means "to redeem." The point of these definitions is that the reclamation for restoration is within the confines of *race*.

The problem with bleeding-heart religions is that they futilely attempt to rescue the entire earth, usually at someone else's expense, and contrary to divine Providence. Their intentions may be good, but that is exactly what the road to hell is paved with. Cliches aside, God makes provision for the future of His people. There is no debate as to whether or not God can accomplish His purposes. The salvation of His elect, Israel, set apart from the alien, is a fate accompli (Romans 8:28-30). Therefore, give diligent attention to the great and precious promises to make your calling and election sure, because there will be con men and race-traitors deceiving and seducing even the very elect, the genetic descendants of Abraham, Isaac and Jacob.

78

If you are a White Christian believer, you have a kinsman redeemer who cares about your deliverance from the burdens of Babylon. The revelation of our "ga'al" is found throughout scriptures.

"For the Lord our God, He it is that brought us up... from the land of Egypt, from the house of bondage... and guarded us in all the way we travelled... and the Lord has driven out all the races... who occupied the land, therefore we will serve the Lord, for He is our God" – Joshua 24:17-18.

A further witness of the ga'al proclaims in Exodus 6:6-8, *"Say to the children of Israel* (the White race)*, I am the Lord, and will bring you out from the burdens of Egypt, and I will rid you out of their bondage* (deliverance) *and will redeem you* (purchase back)... *and with great judgments* (avenger)... *and you shall know that I have brought you out* (rescue)... *and I will bring you to the land... for an heritage* (possession of kin)." Isaiah 53 describes the ransom/sacrifice Christ suffers on our behalf as in verse 5, *"He was wounded for our crimes, bruised for our vices, and with His stripes we are healed."* It continues to tell us about the vicarious price He paid, making intercession for the transgressions of our race (v. 8); when He laid down His soul as an offering for sin, He shall see His *seed* (or race) over time accomplish God's will.

The Law of the kinsman redeemer is found in Leviticus 25:47-55. Here we see the racial aspects of liberation. The redeemer must be a kinsman; *"one of his brethren may redeem him... or any that is near of kin... may redeem him"* (v. 48-49). The idea of a kinsman redeemer in Old Testament times was to help someone in poverty who was unable to redeem their inheritance and redeem his relatives from slavery. Besides this gracious act of redemption towards one's own kind, the kinsman redeemer could also preserve the family line of a deceased male relative by marrying his widow and providing an heir (Deut. 25:5-6).

The Law also stated in Leviticus 25:25, *"when your brother is reduced to poverty, and sells some of his inheritance, if a relative of his brings the redemption for it, then the purchaser shall restore it to his brother."* This was to keep land within a family system of posterity.

Perhaps the most difficult assignment of a kinsman redeemer, or as Numbers 35:19 puts it, a 'revenger of blood' or 'avenger,' was to slay or execute the murderer of his relative. The avenger of blood as in Joshua 20:5 and elsewhere, is the same Hebrew word ga'al (#1350). This Law of God provided order and swift justice within the Israelite society. Today, the White man is robbed of his God-given manhood to hunt down and kill the murderer of his kin. Capital punishment is biblical. *"Moreover ye shall take no satisfaction* (ransom, redemption) *for the life of a murderer, which is guilty of death; but he shall be surely put to death"* –Numbers 35:31. Verses 33-34 explains the reason; so that the land is not polluted; the land cannot be cleansed of the blood that is shed, except by the blood of him who shed it; God said, *"defile not the land which you inhabit, where I dwell, for I the Lord dwell among the children of Israel."* The Law is exclusively applied to the White race.

We know that Jesus never meant to nullify the Law (Mt. 5:17). Therefore, if an individual harms you or your kinfolk criminally, our Christian duty is to see that he is punished to the full extent of the law, in order to make sure he doesn't repeat the crime and inflict harm upon our neighbors. After all, Matthew 19:19 commands us to *"love thy neighbor as thyself."* Not with sentimental affection, but in the sense of a higher moral responsibility. Keep in mind, that race mixing or any other calculation to defile our race is a death curse. A kinsman redeemer will deliver us from such destruction.

Let us now examine carefully the most common Bible story relating to the idea of a kinsman redeemer. Turning to the book of Ruth, we discover types and shadows symbolic of things to come, the advent of Christ. Ruth can be considered typically as Israel, a fore-view of the church; and prophetically, as the bride of Jesus Christ.

Unfortunately, through jewish influence, the book of Ruth has been adulterated in order to rationalize universalism. What comes into question is Ruth's racial background. The pulpit pimps of judeo-Christianity push the unbiblical doctrine of the impure genealogy of Jesus Christ. They say that Ruth, one of His ancestors, was racially a Moabitess, a gentile foreigner who tainted the family tree of our Lord and Savior and therefore changed all of the covenants and promises God made with Israel. With a mixed blood Jesus, they could redeem non-Israelites. The problem with their presumptions is that they regard Ruth as a non-Israelite because she merely resided in the land of Moab. The Bible does not say that Ruth was a non-Israelite. It just says she was a Moabitess. That could infer Ruth was an Israelite resident of Moab who lived there for awhile, or it could mean she descended from the man Moab, the son of Lot, a relative of Abraham. Moab was the same racial blood as Abraham. Even if Ruth descended from Moab, it wouldn't automatically make her a non-White, i.e., non-Israelite.

In Deuteronomy 23:3, the Moabites were excluded from the congregation of Israel because, for the most part, they became race mixers. What the judaizers fail to tell the unsuspecting Christian is the history and timeline of this land named after Moab. With typical chutzpah, jewish scholars (sic) try to tell us that the story of Ruth points to a time long after the age of the judges, even though Ruth 1:1 says, *"Now it came to pass in the days when the judges ruled."* This is like saying that it is raining when the sun shines. But that's how the mind of a jew works.

The time of the judges lasted for about 300 years, from around 1400 BC to 1100 BC, from the death of Joshua to Israel's first king, King Saul. The land of Moab kept that name for many centuries, even after Israel conquered the territory and exterminated the former occupants of the land. After these invasions, the land of Moab was exclusively inhabited by Israelites only. This period was during the life of Ruth. The preposterous assertions that the book of Ruth was to show how a Moabite woman was cordially welcomed into ancient Israel; and became the ancestress of King David and thus brought her racial stock into the pedigree of the Messiah, adds more absurdity to the notion that this story of a racially mixed marriage is told as a protest against the drastic reforms of Ezra and Nehemiah. In their attempt to make all races equal, they must destroy or distort much of the Bible itself.

God excluded the ancient Moabites from entering hallowed ground because they were condemned, as was Sodom (Zeph. 2:9), and shall be trampled down for the dunghill (Isa. 25:10). Since King David and the subsequent kings of Judah did enter the congregation of the Lord, it would have been impossible for them to have had any Moabite blood flowing in their veins. It is only logical that Ruth could not have been a Moabite racially. It is pure rubbish to say then, that Jesus was part Moabite because of Ruth. How dare anyone question God violating His own law!

81

Ruth 1:1 says, *"there was a famine in the land [of Judah]."* If Elimelech and his wife Naomi and two sons left Bethlehem to live on the other side of the Jordan river, why isn't it possible that Ruth and her family did the same thing? It's rather far fetched to suggest that only four people fled from the famine of Judah. If the same race of Moabites were in the land, the same people of whom Balaam tried to curse Israel and destroy, does it make any sense at all, that a century later they would welcome their enemy Israel to live with them and spare them from starvation? Of course, they could not because the Moabites did not live in the land of Moab at that time.

My grandfather came from Ireland to America, but I have not moved back to his homeland, therefore I'm an American, not an Irishman. In like manner, if Ruth's grandparents moved to Moab to escape the famine of Judah, Ruth would be called a Moabitess. Was Moses called an Egyptian because he was one racially; or because he lived in the land of Egypt? Obviously, Moses was an Israelite who had lived in the land of Egypt. Many mistaken identities are made by shoddy Bible scholars because they assume that certain racial groups within a particular geography remain forever static, not even considering that entire populations can be wiped out by war, disease, natural calamities or that thousands of people move and migrate elsewhere. We know such things happened from the historical record.

Let us not have any doubt about Ruth's racial background. She was a pure blooded Israelite and hence, so was Jesus Christ. Ehimelech *"went to sojourn in the country of Moab"* –Ruth 1:1. Notice the explicit wording. If God wanted to convey the idea of integration, it should have read, *"they went to sojourn amongst the people of Moab."* They moved to the geographical area called Moab where there was not one racial Moabite to be found, because the land was now Israelite territory. Ruth couldn't have been of any other race or nation but Israel, for no other race lived there.

The truth of Ruth must be emphatically stressed, otherwise Israel could not have been redeemed by Jesus Christ. The point being, that the nearest of kin is the only one qualified to be a kinsman redeemer. If Christ was not the 'nearest of kin', if He were a half-breed mongrel bastard as the jewish talmud promulgates, if He were not racially White, then He would be ineligible from being

Israel's redeemer. Since Christ did redeem Israel, He must have been the 'nearest of kin.'

"And what one nation in the earth is like thy people Israel, whom God went to redeem to be His own people?" –I Chro. 17:21. Jesus Christ, the Word made flesh, the unblemished lamb, was a racially pure Israelite. He was genetically related to the seed of Abraham (Hebrews 2:16).

The book of Ruth is not an apologetic for miscegenation, nor does it justify antinomian polemics. In other words, the prohibition against interracial marriages were not made void by the dispensational theology of false teachers abolishing God's moral laws. They can attempt to dispense with parts of God's Word, but the only law that was nailed to the Cross was the ordinances of the temple, i.e., animal sacrifices. The blood of Christ became the Passover lamb.

It is the jew, who spoils the lovely picture of the Aryan maiden, Ruth. You see, judaism is predicated on the premise of circumventing the laws of God and thus their malevolent animus towards Christianity's King, Judge and Lawgiver. No wonder Jesus denounced the jew/pharisees when He said, *"In vain do they pay me homage, teaching for doctrines the commandments of men... making the Word of God of non-effect through their tradition"* – Mark 7:7, 13.

In Ruth 1:15 of the jewish manipulated Masoretic text of the KJV and others, it reads that Orpah returned to her people and unto her "gods". The proper rendering should be "God", a singular pronoun meaning the Almighty Creator of Israel, not a plurality of alien deities. Such nonsense would not have been permitted during this era of the judges. See how the jew tinkers with Scripture?

The second chapter of Ruth is the beginning of her romance with Boaz, who is a near kin of Ruth's mother-in-law, Naomi. Verse 20 exclaims that, *"the man is near of kin unto us, he can restore us."* If Ruth were of another race, then Naomi would not have included her as being related by race. The false interpretation from this chapter comes from the word *stranger* in verse 10. It does not prove Ruth was of an alien race. The Hebrew word for stranger is nokriy (#5237), which has a variety of generalized definitions, one of which is *adulterous.* However, there is absolutely no indication

83

whatsoever that Ruth was such. No, she was a stranger in the sense of a foreigner coming from a foreign country.

She must have been a very beautiful White woman whom Boaz informed the local field workers that she should receive special treatment. To think that these local Israelites were xenophobic or hostile to Ruth as some judeo christian writers suggest is without credibility. They were probably intrigued with her being a new member of the community and her same-race countenance coming from a distant land. The hospitality was no doubt voluntary as Boaz told some of the boys not to get too friendly. Boaz is definitely infatuated with Ruth, giving her every courtesy, which would hardly be given to a non-Israelite.

God's law of welfare in an agrarian society was gleaning after the reapers found in Deut. 24:19, where the command says, *"it shall be for the stranger, the fatherless and widows."* Here, the Hebrew word for stranger is geyr (#1616) and means a guest or a travelling Israelite from another country. The reapers gladly observed the law with their new guest in town. This was not just an old custom to be regarded cavalierly; it was from God and His Word/Law. As such, the law forbidding mixed race marriage, which is one of the Ten Commandments, that is, thou shalt not commit adultery (miscegenation), would most certainly be in the mind of Boaz. People have a hard time digesting this today because we don't have a biblical 'law of the land'.

The 36th chapter of Numbers gives the Law of inheritance, and nowhere are other races a consideration. Perhaps the universalists would like to eliminate this chapter as well. Deuteronomy 7:3-4 tells us the principle opposed to race mixing: *"For they* (the racial alien) *will turn away thy son from following me, that they* (Israel) *may serve other gods."*

In chapter three, Ruth is the type of believing Christian who faithfully enters a rest. Naomi is a type symbolizing the Holy Spirit who guides us to our destiny. Boaz is a type of Christ symbolizing the Kinsman Redeemer. Christ is our rest, our destiny. *"There remains a rest to the people of God"* –Heb. 4:9. In the dark of the night, Ruth and Boaz are at rest and he proposes the vows of a kinsman redeemer. He refers to her innate kindness and says, *"I will do to thee all that thou requires, for all the people know you*

are a virtuous woman... it is true that I am thy near kinsman" (v.
11-12). This is a strong parallel to the marriage of the Lamb,
between Christ and His bride, Israel, who *"hath made herself
ready"* –Rev. 19:7.

In the fourth and last chapter, Boaz redeems Ruth by purchasing
the estate of Naomi, and before witnesses at the Gate, took Ruth as
wife to perpetuate the name of the dead. The community
congratulated them with racial overtones expressing best wishes for
an Israelitish progeny, mentioning Rachel and Leah as models for
proliferating our seed-line. Their society was not pluralistic and
they hardly would have been so friendly at such a blatantly illicit
liaison, especially in bringing forth a half-breed offspring to inherit
a sizable amount of land. But the consummation of this marriage
and the birth of Obed was a happy ending to this story. No matter
how some may try to spoil it with innuendo and lies that God
ordained a violation of His divine law.

"And Obed begat Jesse, and Jesse begat David" –Ruth 4:22. Both
Mary and Joseph were descendants of King David. Why would the
genealogy of Jesus be pure except for one case, according to the
liberal minister? Why the charade? If God wanted tainted blood in
the process, why keep and preserve a pristine family tree only to be
corrupted? Why would God incorporate into the Israelite gene pool,
leading through the royal line of David to Christ, a bloodline (Moab)
that he condemned? Why would God impute, *"the possession of
nettles, salt pits and a perpetual desolation"* (Zeph. 2:9) to Moab
and then mix their blood with Israel whom God gave the possession
of land flowing with milk and honey, being salt of the earth and
enjoying a perpetual covenant with God? Why?

During Israel's forty years in the wilderness *"the people began to
commit harlotry with the daughters of Moab"* –Numbers 25:1. The
conspiracy to entice and tempt the men of Israel to mix their seed
with an alien race brought the wrath of God upon them, killing
24,000 in a plague. Does it make any sense, that a century later,
Boaz marries a Moabitess and is not only NOT put to death, but
they are both rewarded and blessed by producing the royal seed of
God's Throne? Is God inconsistent? If this is not enough, a
thousand years later the church in Pergamos was strongly rebuked
for holding this same doctrine of Balaam *"who taught Balak* (the
king of Moab) *to throw a stumbling-block before the sons of*

Israel... to commit fornication (with the alien harlots)" –Rev. 2:14. The answer to all of these questions is that the Holy One of Israel is perfect (Deut. 32:4) and cannot lie (Titus 1:2).

The Lord said, *"I will be the God of all the families of Israel* [not of the world], *and they shall be my people"* –Jer. 31:1. *"And shall not God avenge His chosen race?"* –Luke 18:7. *"The God of the White race chose our fathers"* (Acts 13:7) to be kind after kind, i.e. the same species. *"For God is not the author of confusion"* –I Cor. 14:33. Race mixing is confusion (Lev. 18:23). God does not make a new covenant with any other race than Israel (Heb. 8:10) and He puts the laws of racial purity into their hearts and minds so that the thought of a non-White cohabitating with a White person is repugnant and a violation of our God-given genetic integrity. Miscegenation defiles the bed and dishonors the marriage for which God says He will judge the whoremongers and adulterers and those who adulterate our blood (Heb. 13:4). God is a consuming fire who will make the pulpit pimps of jewish communism charcoal stubble leaving them neither root nor branch and their family tree shall be as ashes under the soles of our feet (Malachi 4:3).

Just as Boaz redeemed Ruth, we have been redeemed also, not with gold or silver, but with the precious blood of Christ (I Peter 1:18-19). Of course, we know now that Christ couldn't be a lawful redeemer for His own people Israel if He wasn't their kin by blood. In Old Testament Hebrew culture, the nearest male blood relative could act as the kinsman redeemer, but he must be related. Some White people might be asking how are we related to Jesus Christ? The New Testament establishes the fact that we are the children of God (Romans 8:16) and our godly motivations, or spirit, is the same as the Spirit of God. Jesus said, *"I was not sent except to the lost sheep of the house of Israel"* (Mt. 15:24) and *"My sheep hear My voice and I know them, and they follow Me"* –John 10:27.

Since Jesus Christ is the Son of God and we are also the sons of God, we become joint-heirs with Christ by virtue of our adoption (Romans 8:15, 17). Jesus is not only our Savior, but also our brother, kinsman redeemer, our closest male blood relative. Romans 8:23 speaks of the *"adoption, to wit, the redemption of our body"* whereby we shall be changed into a glorified body as was Jesus after His resurrection. Adam lost his inheritance, the glorified body of immortality because of sin; and so the entire Adamic race was sold into bondage. Therefore, we need to be delivered from the curse of death.

To ignore the biblical narrative is to ignore the fact that our race disobeyed God at a great price. As long as a sinner or sinful nation owes a debt, he is under the law. When the debt is paid, he is then under grace. The price Israel suffered for whoring after alien gods was God's divorce of her. Jesus Christ then came 2000 years ago, as the Kinsman Redeemer to purchase back His wife, the bride of Christ, so that they were once again the rightful heirs of the promises. Jesus paid the full price for both Israel's and Adam's sin. He purchased all that was lost with His own blood (Acts 20:28). *"In the body of His flesh, through His death, to present you holy and blameless and without charges before our Father in heaven"* –Col. 1:22. *"And because of this, He is the Mediator of the New Covenant, so that His death, for the redemption of our transgressions that were under the first covenant, we have been called to receive the promise of eternal inheritance"* –Heb. 9:15.

The Holy Spirit is given to us as a down payment *"which is the earnest (pledge) of our inheritance (life), until the redemption of the purchased possession"* –Eph. 1:13-14. Paul says we are redeemed from our trespasses and so we should not repeat those trespasses again. Paul says in Romans 6:16-18:

"Don't you know that to whom you yield yourselves slaves for obedience, you are slaves to whom you obey, either of sin resulting in death or of obedience resulting in righteousness? But thanks be to God that though you were slaves of sin, you became obedient from the heart to that form of teaching to which you were delivered. And having been set free from sin, you become the servants of righteousness."

No man can serve two masters. The wages of sin brought the loss of our inheritance (life). But because Jesus has redeemed us from the slave-master Sin, we now serve a new Master, the Redeemer, according to the law of redemption (Lev. 25:53).

The new Master is a near kinsman that loves us and will teach us the ways of righteousness. Redemption does not give us the freedom to do whatever we want. If a man steals $100 and is found guilty by the judge, God's law requires him to pay his victim double, or $200

(Exodus 22:4). If he can't pay it, then he must be sold for his theft. In other words, he must work for a specific amount of time for his victim or for a kinsman who might redeem him. God's justice is restitution, not incarceration. If the sinner refuses to work, he forfeits his life. If our people refuse to hear the Master of our race, they will not enter the Kingdom. If we seek the Kingdom of God and agree to be saved by our Kinsman Redeemer, Jesus Christ, then we need to live by every word proceeding from the mouth of God.

It is no free ride, however. Let us not lose the opportunity our Israelite ancestors had, wandering the wilderness and then entering the Promised Land only to lose it with backsliding. Romans 6:22 puts it like this, *"But now being freed from sin and serving with God, you derive your benefit unto holiness, and the outcome is eternal life."* The idea of holiness here is separation from impurity, i.e. morally, racially and mentally. The thief can no longer steal as he proceeds to prepare and commit his life to Jesus Christ. The new heaven and new earth are not locations, but rather a condition, a state of being with the Lord, in which we will be fully sanctified (set apart for His purposes) in spirit, soul and body as Paul declares in I Thess. 5:23, *"the God of peace Himself may purify you perfectly... and keep you spotless* (without fault) *at the presence of our master Jesus Christ."*

The bride of Christ, *"His wife* (our race) *hath made herself ready... arrayed in fine linen, clean and white, for the fine linen is the righteousness of saints"* –Rev. 19:7-8. This is the vision God gives to the overcomers, the remnant of Israel, a small body of White Christians in this generation. God is using Christian Identity in a mighty way, as an example to the rest of the world. The testimony of our Master is the spirit of prophecy. We are held accountable to be worthy for the day of redemption. No matter how dark things may appear *"grieve not the Holy Spirit of God, whereby you are sealed* (identified) *for a day of redemption"* –Eph. 4:30. For the *"Light shineth in darkness; and the darkness comprehended it not"* –John 1:5.

There will be those with hardened hearts and stiff necks who will not accept the ministry of Kinsman Redeemer. Many are called, but few are chosen. We are now redeemed, but the earnest expectation of the creation waits for the manifestation of the sons of God – total redemption — that will fill all the earth with His grace and glory.

Chapter 14

Who Am I?

Scripture Reading: Matthew 16:13-17

A patient is in a hospital bed coming out of a coma from a head injury; as his vision begins to focus, seeing doctors and nurses he says, "Who am I?" As soon as I decided on this sermon title, I read a description of a movie in the TV guide that said, "An amnesiac struggles to remember who he is while getting experimental therapy at a facility for the terminally ill."

This is a fascinating question, because there are so many answers. One could say their name, their religious affiliation, their nation of birth, etc. We very rarely bump into other Identity Christians, but it happened to me once when I walked into a little T-shirt shop and the proprietor asked me, "Do you know who you are?" And I said without hesitation, "I'm an Israelite" and he just about fell off his chair. Nobody identifies his or her self racially these days, because it's not politically correct. In fact, to announce yourself as a Christian Israelite, hardly anybody would know what you're talking about. And if you don't eat pork, surely you're some sort of converted jew. Oh, if our people only knew who we really are.

Our race has sustained a traumatic head injury and collectively we suffer from spiritual amnesia. Thousands of denominations experiment on your mortal soul; their dead churches even plaster the words 'life' and 'living' on the front edifice. But, it is our faith that restores the focus to clearly remember who we are while we're alive. We are "the children of God" who hath been quickened, becoming the mature "sons of God" and "heirs of the promise."

Every White Christian American and Israelites spread among the nations should ask themselves, "who am I?" because there is a move afoot and has been for some time to not only steal our identity, but to destroy us once and for all.

Jesse Jackson made a career out of the Afrocentric jingoism of "I am somebody," which gave rise and impetus to the next generation of black hip hop and rap music making street thugs and violent nobodies into somebody of importance; and overnight millionaires and flunkies in positions of power. A hyper Affirmative Action that takes revenge and jealousy to stratospheric levels of depravity and corruption.

And if they so happen to live in our society, their legal plunder will resonate with an integrated brainwashed society; their gods of self indulgence and loud noise will be a snare to White children to learn the ways of the heathen. Who am I to declare the mongrel being an inferior creature? I'll answer that with another question from Psalm 2:1, *"Why do the heathen rage and the people imagine a vain thing?"* In other words, other races, having a form of lawlessness in their blood, riot and go wild when White people foolishly think the mongrel can answer the question "who am I?" in the same circumspect manner that we do.

I say we know who we are. We sure aren't the ones who are living luxuriously in a systematic universalism, rewarding parasites that permeate the fabric of society like an indelible stain. The Bible calls the mongrel by many lowly appellations, to wit: locust, caterpillar, gnawing and swarming worms, dogs, swine, goats, snakes etc. I didn't write it, but I know I'm not one of them and they're not one of us. I know that if our nation-race forsakes the Divine Law, these two-legged bipeds become an occupational army; they are, in essence, God's rod of correction.

Who am I? I am ashamed and yet proud of my race. I am sad and yet happy for what we have done. I am anxious and yet patient for what we will do to make things right.

"Then the Lord became jealous for His land and spared His people. Yes, the Lord will answer and say to His people, Behold, I will send you corn, and wine, and oil, and you shall be satisfied... and I will no more make you a disgrace among the heathen... And you sons of Zion, rejoice and be glad in the Lord your God, For He hath given to you the Teacher for righteousness... The Lord says, I will give you back what you lost to the swarming locusts, the hopping locusts, the stripping locusts, and the cutting locusts. It was I who sent this great destroying army against you. Once again you will have all the food you want, and you will praise the Lord your God, who does these miracles for you. Never again will My people be ashamed" –Joel 2:18-19, 23, 25-27.

Who am I? I am not God, but I am of the Great I am. We can distinguish the creature from the Creator when the latter declares, "who I am," in contrast to "who am I." We ask the question and God is the answer.

Probably the most revealing thing about God in the entire Bible, and about us, is found in Exodus 3:13-14:

"And Moses said to God, Behold, when I come to the children of Israel, and shall say to them, The God of your fathers hath sent me to you; and they shall say to me, What is his name? What shall I say to them? And God said to Moses, I AM THAT I AM: And he said, Thus shalt thou say to the children of Israel, I AM hath sent me to you."

God doesn't have to ask Himself, "Who am I?" but rather tells us, "This is who I am." In my humble opinion, I think it is rather absurd and limiting to pigeonhole God with a name as if He were a man. "I AM" is telling us that He is self-existent, unchangeable and incomprehensible. We will not comprehend God by arbitrarily attaching a proper noun to "I AM." Who am I? I'm Mark Downey. Who is God? He's the Great I AM. Are we going to know God better if we arbitrarily name Him as we name ourselves? Or, do our little brains accept the fundamental message of God describing Himself in a simple yet dynamic economy of words? What is more sacred: the ritual of so called "name" repetition, or acknowledging the reality of His Divine Character? Speaking with our mouths, or reverencing with our minds? Who am I to name God, when He told Moses its, "I AM."

The next important thing to understand is that our race has a special relationship with God and this helps us know who we are when we look up at the night sky and ask ourselves, "who am I in this grand cosmos?" We are told that we are made in His image (Gen. 1:26). We were not made as a replica or clone of God, but in His likeness. Adam was immortal, but lost that likeness of eternity. But through the resurrection of the dead, we will once again inherit immortality. The Word of God spoken to Moses was made flesh. Jesus Christ is the incarnation of the Great I AM. In the Gospel of John, Jesus proclaims Himself to be the "Great I AM" seven times (4:26; 6:20; 8:24, 28, 58; 13:19; 18:5). The context of each citation is reinforcing the deity of the Messiah. He said in John 8:58, *"Before Abraham was born, I am."* And the jews knew exactly what He meant and picked up stones to kill Him. Likewise, the enemies of God are intent to kill His followers as well, being that we are like Him.

The word "image" in Gen. 1:26-27 is the Hebrew word tselem #6754 and means 'to shade', as being a resemblance; hence a representative figure; often used to mean similar, as in the phrase 'shades of the past'. Adam was the shades of God, in other words, resembling God's image and having the moral dispositions of God by His Spirit that He placed in Adam. Adam was of the White race because God's color scheme in Scripture portrays godly things only as white or light, never dark or colored.

Some have claimed that Genesis 1:27 refers to the creation of the other races, however Genesis 5 is a parallel account and clearly refers only to Adam. The good intentions of pious churchianity is bankrupt in understanding the Bible as a racial book written in regards to one race only. The other races or sub-species are so insignificant that they are not worth mentioning, albeit the caveat to avoid them. A Ford owner's manual does not discuss Chevrolets. God has decided the exclusions and people have no say in the matter. *"This is the book of the generations of Adam"* –Gen. 5:1.

Paul explains in Romans 8:29 *"For whom He did foreknow, He also did predestinate to be conformed to the image of His Son, that he might be the firstborn among many brethren"* and tells us in the next chapter, Romans 9:3, who his brethren are *"my kinsmen according to the flesh: v. 4 who are Israelites."* The theme of a pure racial lineage runs throughout Old and New Testaments so that the identity of the recipients of God's Word is not lost. However, during history Israel lost their identity and didn't know who they were. Christ knew who the lost sheep of the house of Israel were and that's who He came for (Mt. 15:24). Wolves in sheep's clothing, on the other hand, will say something quite different and identify modern Israel as either jews or anybody who believes, both of which robs the White race of their divine destiny and distorts God's will. The point is, Christ did not fail; and it is still possible for the *lost* to be found.

Christian Identity understands Christ as our Kinsman Redeemer; our brethren who reject this are unbelievers. When the Lord walked the earth, He asked His followers if they knew who He was, which goes directly to the heart of today's message. *"Who do men say **I** the Son of Man **am**?"* It was time to announce to His followers in plain terms His claim to be the Messiah: He would not do this in Judea, where it might cause commotion, and embroil Him with the authorities, but preferred to teach this great truth where He might speak freely without fear of immediate consequences, out of the reach of His persistent adversaries. His public work in Judea and Galilee had reached its end. He had no chance of a hearing if He had made further attempts at teaching. The calumnies of the rabbis had affected the fickle populace, who would willingly have followed a military pretender, but had no heart to follow One whom they were persuaded to regard as a dangerous innovator.

Determined to reveal Himself for such a momentous occasion, He first wanted them to express the mistaken views and scuttlebutt that permeated the region, and then elicit their personal testimony to His straight-forward question, 'who am I?' Thereupon hung the foundation of the Christian Church. Their knowledge of the real nature of Jesus was now being tested. They knew He was more than a man; nor was His appearance an embarrassment to them; they had believed in Him, became His disciples, and were followers of Him; but it was not enough to believe in Him, they must confess Him; both are necessary. Therefore, He does not say, who believes your report, but rather who do you say that I am? You who have been with Me so long from the beginning; you who have heard so many discourses from Me, and have seen so many miracles wrought by Me; and who are to be the teachers of others, to preach My Gospel, and publish My salvation. It was expected of them, that they should know more about Christ than others; and should come to a point of understanding His person and office, and be ready to make a confession of their faith, and give a reason of their hope in Him; and especially such who were to be preachers of Christ to others. They were so well acquainted with Him, as to who and what He is, that they should have no doubt in their minds, ready to declare what they knew and believed of Him with all confidence. Just as we should today; because we can be like Him.

I can imagine Christ thinking, 'after three years and all the fruits of My labor, they think I'm John the Baptist, Elijah, Jeremiah... what made these idiots believe in reincarnation?' We should not tolerate any religion that does not make us fruitful. In Christianity, we have the fruits of the Holy Spirit.

A week before the crucifixion, Jesus was walking along and hungered and saw a fig tree to pick some fruit, but as He got closer the tree was barren and so he cursed that fig tree and it withered. The fig tree represented Israel and more specifically to this parable, "the good and evil figs" of the tribe of Judah. In Christian Identity, we know exactly whom the evil figs represented then, and now. His curse was a symbol of divine judgment against those who would kill Him; it represented the jews in the temple who had made God's Word of none effect by their traditions. Today, it is people who profess to be Christian, but are spiritually barren because they embrace the lies of the jews more than the truths of Christ; they are the whited sepulchers of judeo-Christianity, the bastard reincarnation of judaism.

The fruit of being a Christian is the expression of Jesus Christ. Who am I? I'm an Israelite that confesses Christ, the Anointed Son of the living God; the substance and incarnation of the Everlasting I AM; the perfect God and the perfect man. The only begotten of the Father, of the same nature with Him, being one with Him, and equal to Him. No flesh and blood mortal can reveal who the deity of Christ was and is nor can any man tell me who I am, because it comes from God. Jesus said, "*I AM the way, the truth and the life*" –John 14:6. He also said, "*A thief comes only to steal and to kill and to destroy. I have come so that they may have life and have it in abundance*" –John 10:10.

Who am I? I am abundantly full of life by the grace of God. It's disconcerting that so many of our people today not only cannot answer who they are correctly, but don't care. "*A natural man does not receive the things of the Spirit of God, for they are foolishness to him and he is not able to know, because they are spiritually discerned*" –I Cor. 2:14. A "natural man" is also translated as "unbeliever," "a selfish man," "unspiritual" and "sensual." If we are but mere animals with five senses, it is impossible to perceive that God has some truth for you, to teach you something more than mere survival, to accept a higher power than yourself. If we were created by God in His likeness for a special purpose, we then have an innate supernatural property that all other life forms do not have. This is Spirit. "*God is Spirit, and those who worship Him must worship in spirit and truth.*" Only the spirit of man can commune with the Spirit of spirits.

Who am I in Christ?

You are more than you will ever know.

Our supremacy and status upon the earth (to put it in the enemy's vernacular: White Supremacist) is nothing to boast about, because it is not of our own making, it's of God. If anything, the idea of an elevated race above all the people of the earth (Deut. 7:6) should be a humbling attitude to serve the One who had planned it this way all along. Who am I to shirk and cower from a divine duty? Everything is perfectly on time as scheduled, because God is the Master of time. He alone knows the beginning from the end. I would love nothing more than if our prayers were answered expeditiously, but I'm not in charge of timing. Here's a promise for you: *"I tell you a truth, he who believes in Me* [Christ], *the works that I do, he will do also.* [it doesn't stop there, it gets better] *And he will do even greater works than these, because I go to the Father"* – John 14:12. This is something that has yet to materialize; and it may have to do with a spark that ignites the answer to "who am I?"

Who am I that the King of kings would bleed and die for me? Put into perspective, isn't it a small matter *"When men shall revile you, and persecute you, and shall say all manner of evil against you falsely, for My sake"* –Mt. 5:11. It's prefaced with *"blessed are ye."* It's not easy being Christian Identity.

In my prison ministry, the brethren tell me that their Bibles are sometimes lost accidently on purpose when in transit or simply denied. They can't have hard bound Bibles because it can be used as a weapon... allegedly. My innocent pamphlets have been deemed by some mailroom clerks to be so dangerous that it might cause violence, while jewish, Satanist, voodoo and Islamic jihad materials get a free pass. But, there's one thing that they can't take away from any of us and that's the blood of the Lamb, our Passover sacrifice. And if we go beyond our five senses (our sense of spirit), we can tap into that supernatural healing. Our race has exclusive rights to the New Covenant, whereby the Law is written in our heart and mind. What does that mean? It means we are vessels of honor. It means we are babes in the loving hands of our Father given the provisions of His Spirit to do His will. What an amazing grace for such spoiled brats and ingrates.

The precursor to Christian Identity was British Israelism, and one of their teachings was that America was represented by the tribe of Manasseh, which ironically means 'forgetful.' We should be called the United States of Amnesia, as we are treated like lab rats by our captors; and every precaution is taken to maintain the illusion of those who say they are Israel, but are the synagogue of satan. Likewise, we live in a multicultural country, because we are no longer a nation-race, where social engineers inculcate a death wish in a non-stop culture war. Who are we? We are dumb and blind.

I attended a symposium in which the speakers were warning the audience about radical White groups. During the Q&A we made our presence known that we were White and radical. Afterwards, this big black buck comes up to me and asks, "Are you a White Supremacist?" And I said, "Yes, we are supremely stupid for losing our Beulah Land." He seemed a bit stunned and just walked away. I don't think our people are stupid, but I think they've been stupefied. What do you expect when our water is fluoridated, our air is chem-trailed, and our food is Frankensteined? The schools, media and churches work in concert to opiate the White race, to experiment with our progeny and to marginalize life and death itself without God.

Jewish communism didn't work too well in the old Soviet Union and one can almost see Russia today being more Christian than America. That's because The Bolshevik Revolution was financed by jews right here in America and the closest they came to being exposed was with Joe McCarthy... over 60 years ago! Esau-Edom is still here like maggots on a skeleton. Who are we? We're the dry bones of Israel. Jacob is going through a time of trouble as never before.

It's hard to keep up with the daily wars and rumors of war. We've settled in our Beulah Land where we can move no more (II Sam. 7:10), but that doesn't seem to prevent others from moving in on us. And there shall be enmity between us and them (Gen. 3:15). *"For I would not, brethren, that you should be ignorant of this mystery, lest you should be wise in your own conceits; that blindness in part is happened to Israel, until the fullness of the Gentiles comes in"* –Romans 11:25.

You and I know that the KJV continues to keep people ignorant of what this verse is really saying. The mystery is the racial identity of who we are, because we're both Israel and the "Gentiles" (which just means nations, not non-jews). The mystery of the gentiles (in this verse) begs the question: which nations? It's the nations of non-Israelites or non-Whites, again not non-jews, because jews may look White, but they are mongrels and they're behind the alien invasion of America. Our people cannot see this prophecy, because they don't know who they are. However, the fulfillment is that the blindness will go into remission when we are thoroughly overwhelmed by mongrelization. The eye-opener, being 'better late than never', shows the love and mercy of the God of segregation. Unfortunately, it has to get worse before it gets better to convince even the most hardened egalitarian heart, that only through divine intervention will we be released from the final captivity of Babylon.

To many it will seem impossible to reverse the insanity of racial reconciliation: the browning of America has won and the White race is doomed for extinction. But hold on; right after verse twenty-five, it says, *"And so all* [believers? no...] *Israel shall be saved: as it is written, There shall come out of Zion the Deliverer, and shall turn away ungodliness from* [believers? no...] *Jacob: For this is My covenant to them, when I shall take away their sins."* One of those sins was the "believer" who thought race mixing was Christian; and who warred against God and their own people.

You know, the Word of God is likened unto water, and Ezekiel had this vision of our people being dry as a bone; the kind you see in a scorching desert with not a strand of flesh, dehydrated to the marrow, not even a speck of meat left for bugs to pick at. It's really quite a graphic depiction of Israel in prophecy. And the Lord said to him:

"Can these bones live? And I replied, O Lord only you know. Again He said to me, Preach to these bones, and say to them, Dry bones listen to the message of the Living Life. This is what the Mighty Lord proclaims to these bones, I will bring a wind [Spirit, breath, CPR] *to you and you shall revive! I will also put sinews* [tendons] *on you, and cause flesh [muscle] to cover you, and cover you with skin, and put breath into you, when you will revive, and learn that I AM the Life... So I proclaimed as He ordered me, and the wind came to them and they revived, and stood on their feet, a very, very great army!"* (Ezek. 37:3-7, 10 FF).

Do you think Yale's 'Skull & Bones' Club would want any of that muscle? No, they're a death cult and their bones-men, like crypto-jew John Kerry, go around making war and rumor of wars. Be afraid, be very afraid of the darkness in high places? No. *"Do not fear them which kill the body, but are not able to kill the life. But rather fear the One who is able to destroy both the life and the body in Gehenna!"* –Mt. 10:28. Who am I? I'm a God fearing White man standing in the grace of God. No human power can restore the bones of man, buried in the ground, to life. God alone can cause a dead man's bones to revitalize and become whole again. If you're despondent about all of the doom and gloom brought to you courtesy of media whores and pulpit pimps, then *"look up, and lift up your heads; because your redemption draweth nigh"* –Luke 21:28. This vision of Ezekiel was given to encourage us in the latter days, which predicts both the restoration after the captivity/slavery to the final Babylon, and recovery from the Edomite occupation of our land. It was also a clear intimation of the resurrection and conversion of the most hopeless sinners to Christ. Let us look to Him who will at last open our graves, and bring us forth to judgment, that He may now deliver us from sin, and put his Spirit within us, and keep us by His power, through faith, unto salvation. *"For if we have hope in Christ in this life only, we are of all men most miserable"* –I Cor. 15:19. Who am I? I'm the recipient of, and believer in, the Word made flesh, who is my Kinsman Redeemer, who created Adam in His likeness and promises me and you eternal friendship.

Jesus lives in us. Time and again Scriptures say, *"I will be their God, and they will be My people."* Who is He talking about? Everybody upon the earth? Jeremiah 31:1 says, *"I will be the God of*

99

all the families of [the earth? no...] *Israel, and they will be My people."*

"What agreement does the temple of God have with idols? For we are a temple of the Living God, as God has said, I will dwell in them, and walk among them, and I will be their God, and they will be My people. Therefore come out from among them, and be ye separate, saith the Lord, and touch not the unclean thing; and I will receive you" –II Cor. 6:16-17. This isn't talking about pigs or dirty dishes, but rather race mixing. The stranger and his strange gods have no place in Israel. But, if you believe the mongrel is to be included in the Kingdom, you have not yet separated yourself from the unclean; you're not a true believer.

Who am I to think I am sovereign; to think I can contradict Scripture and decide for myself what is right or wrong? My life is not my own. *"What? You don't know that your body is the temple of the Holy Spirit which is in you, which you have from God and you are not your own? For you have been bought with a price; therefore glorify God in your body, and in your spirit, which are God's"* –I Cor. 6:19-20.

"You, however, are not in the flesh, but in the Spirit, since the Spirit of God lives in you. But if anyone does not have the Spirit of Christ, he does not belong to Him" –Romans 8:9. That's the difference between our race and all others. *"That which is born from flesh is flesh, and that which is born from The Spirit is spirit"* –John 3:6. Only Adam was given the 'breath of life' otherwise known as the Spirit of God, meaning that we were not only born on earth, but begotten of God. Our thoughts are affected by the world, but that is the object of our overcoming the flesh in the likeness of Christ. Is it time for you to know who you are and walk into your destiny and to think and to live like "the royal priesthood," "ambassadors of Christ," "a chosen race," and "God's covenant people."

The Lord said, *"**I am** the light of the world: he that followeth Me shall not walk in darkness, but shall have the light of life"* –John 8:12. In Mt. 5:14, the Lord proclaims, *"You are the light of the world"* and in verse 16, *"Let your light so shine before men, that they may see your good works, and glorify your Father which is in heaven."* We Identity Christians have the key to unlock the renewing of our minds with a vast, untapped potential to advance the Kingdom with the gifts of our calling. We are Christians who must detoxify from the sorceries of churchianity and be disciplined in the supernatural mind of Christ.

It's kind of a funny thing doing what I do: I have this compelling magnetism to impart something beyond my own wisdom, which automatically flows from my brain to you. I don't have voices in my head, but I hear a non-audible type of spiritual GPS that takes the lead, which I follow. I have confidence that it is God who lives in me.

The funny thing is that this Christian Identity Truth is milk and honey for some people, whereas with others it just does not compute. *"The wicked mock God and say, Hurry up and do something! We want to see what you can do. And let the purpose of the Holy One of Israel draw near and come, that we may know it!"* –Isaiah 5:19. They want the truth and they want it now.

A couple of weeks ago I was too busy to delve deep into my head to even ask "who am I?" So how hard do you think it is to get into somebody else's head? We're not anything special other than what God has specialized us in at any given moment. I Peter 2:9 says we are a chosen race and a peculiar people; and the NIV goes so far as to say: *"God's special possession, that you may declare the praises of Him who called you out of darkness into His wonderful light."*

"For I say, through the grace given unto me, to every man that is among you, not to think of himself more highly than he ought to think; but to think soberly, according as God hath dealt to every man the measure of faith" –Romans 12:3. There's a difference between messengers and a message. We wouldn't have Christianity today if it weren't for the messengers willing to die for the message. They cared about who we are.

"For now we see through a glass, darkly; but then face to face: now I know in part; but then shall I know even as also I am known" –I Cor. 13:12. We see things imperfectly, like puzzling reflections in a mirror, but eventually we will see everything with perfect clarity. True Israel's knowledge of itself is partially blind and incomplete. Our people are processed like cattle through the filters of political correctness. But our destiny is to be complete Christians, just as God knows us completely. After all, He knows us better than we do.

You want the truth? You can handle the truth! The truth will literally make you free; it will separate the wheat from the chaff, the dross from the gold. It's time to take the trash out. Why is it that one of the hardest things for a White person to believe is that they are Israel and not the jews? I don't have an easy answer, but I think it has something to do with avoiding the question, "who am I?" If you love those who hate the Lord, then you don't know yourself; and if you promote this misguided notion, you are the *"blind leading the blind into a ditch."*

These same people accuse me of leading the flocks astray. But, it's just the same old garbage of cognitive dissonance where their beliefs are set in concrete. Well, no matter how set in their beliefs, there's a divine shakedown on the way. When God spoke from Mount Sinai His voice shook the earth, but now He makes another promise: *"Once again I will shake not only the earth but the heavens also"* – Heb. 12:26. The ultimate reference is what is seen dimly afar off in so many of the prophetic visions i.e. the final dissolution of the whole present order of things, to be succeeded by the Kingdom of eternal righteousness. It's not talking about God's abode in the heavens, but rather man's elevated authority in law and government. This expression, *"Yet once more, denotes the removing of those things which can be shaken, as of created things, so that those things which cannot be shaken may remain"* –Heb. 12:27.

God is a racist. I am a racist. Let true Israel be warned of forgetting, denying, or worse... hating the covenants of the Lord their God. Who am I? I am loved of Jesus Christ. *"We are more than conquerors through Him that loved us"* –Romans 8:37.

Appendix A:

Is White Supremacy Scriptural?

It is curious as to how this expression "White Supremacy" has become such a bugaboo, how it invokes images of some sort of exaggerated cult and how the average citizen reacts to the utterance of this phrase. We know the enemy perverts language and is the author of confusion, therefore it would behoove us to research words that are so loosely bandied about that are causing us so much trouble. From my original 1847 Webster's dictionary, the definitions of the following words: **Supremacy** – state of being supreme or in the highest station of power; highest authority or power; as the supremacy of the king of Great Britain; or the supremacy of parliament. **Supreme** – highest in authority; holding the highest place in government or power. **Superior** – [from super, above] 1. higher, upper, more elevated in place 2. higher in rank or office, more exalted in dignity 3. higher or greater in excellence, surpassing others in greatness, goodness or value of any quality; as a man of superior merit, bravery, talents, understanding, accomplishments 4. being beyond the power or influence of, too great or firm to be subdued or affected by.

The word supremacist was not in the 1847 Webster's Dictionary. From Webster's 7th new Collegiate Dictionary 1972 the definitions of the following words: **Supremacist** – an advocate or adherent of group supremacy [a white ~]. Supremacy – the quality or state of being supreme; the position of being first (as in rank, power or influence), implies superiority over all others, the idea of domination over one another. **1. Superior** – 1. situated higher up, 2. rank, quality, importance, 3. courageously or serenely indifferent (as to something painful, disheartening or demoralizing), 4. greater in quantity or numbers, excellent of its kind, better. **2. Superior** –

103

1. one who is above another in rank, station, or office esp. the head of a religious house or order, 2. one that surpasses another in quality or merit.

Now let us direct our attention to the Bible that indicates an interesting parallel with the preceding dictionary definitions, without having to resort to twisting or doing violence to scripture. There is an over-abundance of verses that declare God has a chosen people. Psalm 33:12, Blessed is the nation... and people whom He hath chosen for His own. John 15:19, If ye were of the world, the world would love his own... but I have chosen you out of the world, therefore the world hateth you. Also Psalm 105:43, 106:5, Mark 13:20, Acts 13:17, Deut. 10:15, 14:2.

Additionally, the election of God points to divine specifications: I Peter 1:1-2, "to the strangers (Israelites) scattered... the elect according to the foreknowledge of God." Romans 9:11, "For the children (of Israel) being not yet born, not having done anything good or evil, that the purpose of God according to the election might stand." If this isn't enough prejudice, God further elevates His Chosen to be above (remember the definition of superior?) other people. Deuteronomy 7:6, "For thou art an holy people unto the Lord thy God, the Lord thy God hath chosen thee to be a special people unto himself, **ABOVE** all people that are upon the face of the earth." Exodus 19:5, "ye shall be a peculiar treasure unto me, **above all people**." Also Deut. 7:14, 14:2, 26:19, 28:1, 13; II Samuel 22:48-49, Psalm 45:7, Micah 4:1, Isaiah 2:2.

So then, what happens to the non-Israelites? Psalm 47:3, *"He shall subdue the people under us, and the nations under our feet."* This is beginning to sound like God is a racist!

Nothing has raised man to the peaks of creativity or lowered him to depths of destruction than the dual notion of racial similarity and differences. Both have biological overtones for the individual and groups of individuals. It is the inevitable characteristics of one group that differentiates from another. Whether you like it or not, this is the reality of race in a nutshell. Race goes far beyond the color of skin. The concept of race encompasses so many facts and fictions, love and hate, reason and unreason that are more easily sensed than understood.

Webster's definition of racism is "a belief that race is the primary determinant of human traits and capacities and that racial differences produce an inherent superiority of a particular race." Belief implies assent to expressing the idea or putting the belief into action, in politics, religion, art, business, community, home, et cetera. The racism of a racial group will change from a static to a dynamic character when it becomes the victim of oppression and the peaceful security of the society is at risk. This is a natural confrontation in nature, an instinct for survival.

Ironically, anti-racism feeds its own agenda in the reverse by practicing racism vicariously by adopting the cause of every race but their own. Racism is a form of group morale, providing a protective psychic shell for the most defenseless and defensive peoples, and a responsibility for an aggressive fighting spirit. The race is an extension of the family and death comes easier to those who believe they are dying for their own kind. Racism may be the most compelling force or factor in the rise and fall of civilizations. Consider the distortions of history which avoid racism altogether or glibly treat it as a disease rather than as a basic element of our God given genetic memory. Our enemies would have us forget who and what we are and erase the past. COULD IT BE THAT THEY HAVE CORRECTLY CALLED US WHITE SUPREMACIST AND HAVE GOTTEN US TO REJECT THIS TRUTH ABOUT OURSELVES?

Use of the phrase 'White Supremacist' became popularized in the 1960's referring to opponents of the civil rights movement and desegregation. In order to insure their own superiority, the defamation liberals employ silence and confuse any ideas about White people being the true Israelites of the Bible ... to the point of getting us into denial and a guilt complex similar to the clever jewish psychology of 'holocaust' hysteria and the repercussions of challenging their allegations. They go berserk when the White man lives above their (man made) laws, obeying God's Laws, because the kingdom of Heaven is here and now and Christ is our Sovereign, and we are willing to die for the cause of Christ. They will associate White Supremacist with criminal activity or mental illness. The mark of a White Supremacist isn't false pride, it is virtue; and does not encompass the whole of Christendom, but rather a radical remnant that probably wouldn't call themselves White Supremacist inasmuch that they have a humble spirit and live modest lives. These are the 'salt of the earth' that race-mixers ridicule and malign.

Christ died for His people, His sheep, His race, not the non elect. Otherwise, everyone would be saved and we know that is simply contrary to scripture. You see, God has made the good guys and the bad guys for His plan and purposes whether it meets with your approval or not. Jesus told His disciples to stay away from the heathen and to go only to Israelites (Matthew 10:5-6). The good news is that the White race is the lost sheep of the house of Israel for which Christ came, not jews, not the pseudo church and certainly not just anybody or any race that merely believes.

We Whites are the recipients of the Old and New Covenant and those who would spiritualize Israel away make God a liar. The prophecies given to a physical seed-line become null and void. If the Bible is addressed to Israel only (and it is), then when the word 'every' or 'all' is used, it means every or all Israelites. All are one in Christ means all Israelites. Only His sheep hear His voice. How do the sheep demonstrate supremacy? We rise above un-Christian behavior, we live as Christ our example and we walk in His steps. Christ was the epitome of a White Supremacist being the Chief Shepherd showing us the Way. Why would a White Supremacist insist upon being above? Because it is the believer's union with Christ now and hereafter. It says in Colossians 3:1, if ye then be risen with Christ, seek those things which are above, where Christ sits on the right hand of God; verses 9-10, put off the old man... put on the new man, whereby we are renewed in knowledge, v.11, where there is nothing among various Israelites, but Christ (the whole) is all, and in all (in all races?)... the context is v.12, put on therefore, as the elect of God... the following virtues of Christian Israelites. Can anybody be the elect? Isaiah 45:4 says, "Israel mine elect" same as Deuteronomy 7:6 and I Peter 1:1-2 called the scattered strangers 'the elect'.

White Supremacists are highly principled by heavenly design, impervious to brainwashing, having the full armor of God to resist spiritual wickedness in high places. These satans in the beast governments have declared war against White Supremacists because the light of the world is so opposite and contrary to their dark philosophies and laws. *These shall make war with the Lamb* (Revelation 17:14) *and the Lamb* (Christ) *shall overcome them...* with His *called, chosen and faithful.*

White Supremacists are superior if they practice the righteousness of Christ (Zeph. 3:13, 19). Is not a truth teller superior to a liar? The Ferrar Fenton Bible puts it this way in Haggai 2:7, *the Desired* (i.e., Christ and Christian White Supremacists) *of all nations* (of all Israelite nations) *will come and fill this house with splendor* (elevated excellence); v. 13-14 *when a defiled person* (a non-White Supremacist, spiritually or physically dead, an alien or heathen) *touches anything consecrated* (the holy being separated from the profane), *it becomes defiled,* v. 22-23 God will destroy the inferior defiled heathen because He has chosen the purity of our race (Matthew 5:8, Titus 1:15).

We need to understand the words: man/mankind, people, neighbor, brothers/brethren, nation(s), gentile and stranger(s). The words human, humanity, humanism and humanitarian are not in the Bible. The word hue means color, therefore hue-man means a colored entity. It is interesting to note that white is not part of the rainbow or natural spectrum. The Adamic race was a special creation. The other races were pre-Adamic. The special relationship of God and mankind is within the family of Adam, not all of humanity or the various non-Adamic races.

What would Christianity be without the White race? The White Supremacists are the standard-bearers of Christianity. Jeremiah 51:12 says, *"set up the standard upon the walls of Babylon, make the watch strong, set up the watchmen, prepare the ambushes."* The remnant (White Supremacists) of Israelite Christians always awake under captivity before others, because we are the called out ones of God. It is satan, in a national sense, or wicked government that the remnant actively tries to withdraw from; those withdrawing are called separatists, racists, bigots or White Supremacists. Could it be that we are above them because they keep lowering the standards of everything? False prophets say that if you don't believe Christ loves all people, you're a racist. Yet Christ said, *"bring mine enemies before me and slay them"* (Luke 19:27). Don't think He came to send peace on earth. He came to deliver a sword and division (Matthew 10:34, Luke 12:51). Evangelism fails if it only saves to send people to a pie in the sky heaven or barbecue pit of hell. What about saving our race and nation?

At one time 'Christian' was synonymous with the White race, but it has become a racially homogenized religion with every sort of perverted denomination (a nice word for cult) imaginable. Why do we have to respect and tolerate other so called religions? The first amendment to the Constitution deals only from a Christian perspective. It will not work otherwise. The diatribe against White Supremacists is used to circumvent our birthright destiny. You'll see in Micah 3:1-3 that the racial melting pot is like a horrid cannibal's stew. The melting pot people would eliminate any and all standards that would identify the tribes of Israel. They are out to destroy all of White civilization and culture. We are reviled and despised because we have the Lord within us to execute His Laws. No other race has this assignment. The order of the New World Order is self explanatory: 'they' are ordering us to bow down to their rule, law and authority.

Are we going to rise to the occasion, because our national house has fallen to the depths of the present Babylonian cesspool? Are we going to rise up and come out of our captivity? Chapter eleven of Romans speaks of us (Israel) being down but not forgotten, v.2 God hath not cast away His people and God reassured Elijah that he was not alone, v. 4-5. Could it be that we have a parallel remnant of Israelites today; a special election of White Supremacists who deny the image of Baal? We know that the majority of Israelites are blind because of the riches of the world. Don't you have to be color blind these days to be politically correct? But Paul speaks exclusively of them, v. 14, which are my flesh or racial kindred.

Verses 16-24 talks about an olive tree and cutting (with a sword perhaps!) and grafting branches. This olive tree is symbolic of Israel. Verse 16 *"if the firstfruit be holy, the crop is also; if the root is holy, the branches are also."* Some branches were cut off for unbelief and a wild branch (the lost tribes) were grafted in; the root accepts the wild one through the branch's faith. It is not the branch that accepts the root for life. God's pruning of the olive tree maintains the Life of the tree for His purposes. The lesson here is that you cannot graft on an apple branch to an olive tree any more than you can say that the other races pertain to God's special election of Israel. Romans 11:29, *"For the gifts and calling of God are without change"* (it's irrevocable), v.32 *"that He might have mercy on all"* (the context is v. 26, **all Israel** – not all races).

Finally, what is revealed to us about race in the 'end times'? Jesus likened it to the days of Noah and Lot (Luke 17:26-30). The dominant sin of that day was the promiscuous interracial marriages bringing with it strange gods and lawlessness. Compared with Noah's flood we can witness the rising tide of color in our midst today. We are flooded with multi-cultural diversity, ethnic pluralism, rainbow coalitions and a multitude of parasites on a host nation that has been spiritually lobotomized. What is our flood? The serpent cast out of his mouth water as a flood (Revelation 12:15). The great whore of Mystery Babylon sits upon many waters, which is to say many races, multitudes, nations and tongues (Revelation 17:1,15). When the enemy shall come in like a flood, the Spirit of the Lord shall lift up a standard against him (Isaiah 59:19). What is our standard? That ole Adamic supremacist Noah had an ark to save his racially pure family. What is our ark to save us from drowning in a sea of antichrist heathen? What was the precious contents of the ark of the covenant? Was it not the testimony of God and His Law? We are superior by the New Covenant. God supernaturally put His Law into our heart, mind, soul and chromosomes. We were created to serve God. In order to serve we must invoke and unlock the power of divine mandates, lest we perish in ignorance and shameful concessions of equality.

Appendix B:

Identification Marks of Israel

In John 10:38 and 20:29-31, Jesus, in essence, told them even if you don't believe His simple proclamation and doubt His Word, believe the works (signs and miracles) that you may know He is the Son of God. Likewise, being consistent with Jesus' reply for proof, the true identity of Israel can only be claimed by those who fulfill the signs or marks, not just taking somebody's word for it.

1. a great and mighty nation: Gen.12:2, 18:18, Deut. 4:7-8
2. named "Great": Gen. 12:2
3. be blessed of God: Gen.12:2
4. will be a blessing to other nations/races: Gen. 12:2-3
5. other nations affected depending on how they deal with Israel: Gen. 12:3
6. a great multitude (population): Gen. 13:16 and 22:17
7. Egyptian captivity and deliverance (precedent for chastisement): Gen. 15:13- 14
8. given land in Middle East: Gen. 15:18
9. become many nations: Gen. 17:4
10. a company or commonwealth of nations: Gen.35:11
11. descendants to be kings and rulers: Gen. 35:11
12. land of Canaan theirs for an everlasting possession: Gen.17:8
13. mark of circumcision: Gen. 17:10-11
14. keep the way of the Lord, do justice and judgment: Gen. 18:19
15. keeping sabbath a sign forever: Ex. 31:13
16. possess the gates of their enemies: Gen.22:17
17. Israel chief among the nations: Jer. 31:7
18. only Israel is custodian of God's Word: Ps. 147:19, Is. 59:21
19. possess God's laws: Deut. 33:4

20. blessed above all people when obedient to His law: Deut. 28
21. judged for disobeying: Deut. 28:15-68, Amos 3:1-2
22. control of the seas: Num. 24:7, Ps. 89:25
23. God's servant race: Is. 41:8
24. will possess God's Holy Spirit: Is. 44:3, 59:21, Hag. 2:5
25. a missionary nation: Is. 49:6, 66:19
26. great agricultural wealth: Gen. 27:28, Deut. 8:7-9, 33:13-14
27. a land of great mineral wealth: Deut. 8:9, 33:15-16, Gen. 49:25
28. Israel brings glory to God: Is. 46:23, 49:3
29. Israel to be God's glory: Is.46:13, 60:1-2
30. God's instrument in destroying evil: Jer. 51:20, Dan. 2:34-35
31. to be God's witnesses: Is. 43:10
32. will demonstrate praise and expertise: Is. 43:21, Micah 5:7
33. a multitudinous seed: Gen. 13:16, 24:60 dust 15:5 stars 22:17 sand
34. God of the Bible to be God of Abraham's descendants: Gen. 17:7
35. to be God's inheritance/heritage: I Kings 8:53, II Sam. 7:23
36. to rule over others: Gen. 27:29, Deut. 15:6
37. Israel to have power with God and men: Gen:32:28
38. a righteous nation guarding truth: Is. 26:2
39. Israel to be a nation forever: II Sam. 7:16,24,29 I Chron. 17:22-27
40. to be heir of the world: Romans 4:13
41. Israel to have all the land needed: Deut. 32:8
42. an undefeated nation, protected by God: Is. 54:17, Lev. 26:6-8, Micah 5:8-9
43. Israel to be God's battle axe to destroy evil: Jer. 51:19-20
44. Israel's home invincible from outside forces: II Sam. 7:10, Is. 41:11-13
45. a just nation: Gen. 18:19, Lev. 19:15, Deut. 1:17
46. possess the wealth of the earth: Gen. 27:28, 49:25-26
47. possess the heritage of the heathen: II Sam. 22:44, Ps. 2:8, 111:6
48. Israel to be envied and feared: Deut. 2:25, 4:8, 28:10
49. shall lend to other nations: Deut. 15:6
50. kind to the poor / brethren: Deut. 15:7, Ps. 72:4
51. to free kindred slaves and political prisoners: Is. 42:7, 49:9, 58:6
52. Joseph's descendants blessed above rest of Israel: Gen. 49:22-26, Deut. 33:13-16

53. Out of Judah would come the rulers of Israel: Gen. 49:10
54. the throne of David is a perpetual monarchy: Ps. 89:35-37, Jer. 33:17, II Sam. 7:13,16, II Chron. 13:5
55. 12 tribed Israel to lose all trace of her lineage: Is.42:19, Hosea 1:9
56. divorced and dispersed, they could not return to Palestine: Hosea 2:6
57. blind to their identity: Is. 29:10-11, Romans 11:7-8,25
58. Israel to spread abroad in all directions: Gen. 28:14, Deut. 33:17, Is. 27:6
59. Israel to have a new home: II Sam. 7:10, I Chron. 17:9
60. new home is not Palestine, but the isles of the sea: Is. 24:15, 49:1, Jer. 31:10
61. Israel's new home northwest of Palestine: Is. 49:12, Jer. 3:18, 31:8
62. would occupy and live in the islands and coasts: Is. 49:1,3, 51:5, Jer. 31:7- 10
63. would colonize, spreading abroad: Gen. 49:22, Ps. 2:8, Zech. 10:8-9, Is. 26:15, 27:6
64. colonize the desolate places: Is. 35:1, 43:19-20, 49:8, 54:3
65. Israel to lose a colony (America from England) then expand: Is. 49:19-20
66. will irrigate the deserts: Is. 58:11
67. will build the waste places: Is. 58:12
68. will be a maritime nation, command of the seas: Num. 24:7, Ps. 89:25
69. will receive strangers and refugees (kinsmen living abroad): Lev. 19:34, Is. 11:10,14:1, 56:6-8
70. Israel to have a change in name: Is. 65:15, Hosea 2:17
71. Israel to be called by a new name: Is. 62:2
72. Israel named after Isaac's son i.e.. Saxon: Gen. 21:12, Romans 9:7
73. Israel to be called the sons of God i.e.. accept Christ: Hosea 1:10
74. were to be called by the name of God i.e.. Christian: Num. 6:22-27, Rev. 3:12
75. Israel to have a new language (English): Is. 28:11, Zeph. 3:9
76. Israel to come under new covenant: Jer. 31:33, Heb. 8:10
77. 'brith' means covenant, 'ain' means land (Britain- covenant land)
78. 'ish' means man (British- covenant man)

79. Joseph's coat of many colors, forerunner of Scottish plaid – Gen. 37:3
80. the cubit of the Pyramid, Noah's ark, Moses tabernacle and Solomon's temple is the English 25 inch measurement
81. the population of the wilderness with Moses and the original 13 American colonies was 3 million
82. inscribed on the Liberty Bell is Leviticus 25:10
83. like Joseph, lost Israel is powerful yet unrecognized by brothers, giving bread to the world
84. the coronation ceremony for British royalty same as King David: II Kings 11:12, II Chron. 13:5
85. the coronation stone of British royalty is the stone of Israel which Jacob used for a pillow and set up as a pillar: Gen. 28:19,22, 35:14-15
86. Joseph was hated as we are today by the rest of the world: Gen. 37:4, 49:23
87. Joseph sold into slavery as we are put into economic bondage: Gen. 37:28, Jer. 30:8
88. the descendants of Joseph spread abroad: Deut.33:17
89. today we declare ourselves to our brethren as Joseph did: Gen. 45:1,3
90. America shall blossom as the rose in the desert: Is. 35:1
91. eagle with outstretched wings national emblem of U.S.A.: Is. 18:1, Rev. 12:14
92. our early ambassadors had to travel over sea: Is. 18:2
93. a nation meted out (measured, surveyed land by boundaries): Is. 18:2
94. whose land the rivers have spoiled (to cleave or specifically quartered): Is. 18:2
95. people scattered , tall and peeled like smooth trees (no beards) and terrible from their beginning fits the Indians wasted by continual wars and the later White Americans
96. the land beyond (west of) the rivers of Ethiopia is America: Is. 18:1
97. "In God we trust" became our national motto passed by Congress, becoming law of the United States of America, July 30, 1965
98. Israel's sojourn into the wilderness (America): Hosea 2:14
99. Israel to be a people saved by the Lord: Is. 43:9-12, 44:1-3
100. As the end of the age draws near, travel and search for knowledge and information shall be increased: Daniel 12:4 much more so in America

When you consider that there are more than 100 recognized nations in the world today, the mathematical odds against all of these identification marks being fulfilled by just one small group of nations, all of the same blood, is billions to one. But since it has happened, that the marks of Israel have been fulfilled by the Anglo-Saxon and kindred people, do you think it mere accident or coincidence? If we are not Israel, then what has happened to all of God's prophecies? It certainly is not the Jews or anybody else that even comes close to matching the biblical descriptions. The White race alone fits every piece of the puzzle.

Made in the USA
Las Vegas, NV
15 March 2024

87224244R00069